The Pavilion Book of
PAVILIONS

C000163118

The Pavilion Book of
PAVILIONS

Jonathan Rice

—●—

Photographs by Paul Barker

Foreword by Tony Lewis

PAVILION

First published in Great Britain in 1991 by
PAVILION BOOKS LIMITED
196 Shaftesbury Avenue, London WC2H 8JL

A CIP catalogue record for this book is
available from the British Library

ISBN 1 85145 5531

10 9 8 7 6 5 4 3 2 1

Printed and bound in Italy by L.E.G.O.

*Frontispiece: Shobrooke Park; page 4
Saltwood; page 112 Holmfirth.*

Contents

Foreword

DURING THE Second World War my playground was a rotting, disused cricket pavilion on the Gnoll ground in Neath in Glamorgan. Hellbent boys crawled wild underneath it between brick supports or scrambled up through holes in the wooden floor to make camp fires for heating a billycan of water all the better to boil spiders.

I did not know then that one of my cigarette card collection, the neckerchiefed C. F. Walters of Worcestershire and England, had many times in his schoolboy days walked down the gentle flight of steps to bat for Neath.

The commercial age has changed the aspect of Neath's pavilion: it had facial surgery which went awfully wrong.

Pavilions of one's youth stay under the skin. Strangely enough, Lord's, when I first represented the Royal Air Force there in 1958, did not have the expected impact. It was too big to touch me: there was no one to bump into on the wide stairs. The large dressing room had chairs and sofas yards apart around the sides, and it had its own balcony. Going out to bat, I recall the stairs had a rubbery smell: through the Long Room my head was down so I never really had a good look at it.

In my early days pavilions meant separation. I was an amateur for the first seven years of my first-class career and often ended up in a different dressing room from the professionals. We did not always share the same dining room. As professionals got stuck into their cottage pie in their own dining-room, amateurs sipped a sherry and gave orders to uniformed waitresses in the committee quarters.

Pavilions abroad are either splendidly old Empire with verandahs and plumed waiters in white 'tackies' bearing long whisky sodas or they are not pavilions at all. When I walked out to toss in my first Test match in Delhi in 1973 I found myself walking into sunshine along a sort of chicken run conduit to the field. More like footballers, Ajit Wadekar and I appeared to come out of the belly of the pavilion.

Since then I have always loved best those pavilions which add theatre to the game by creating a staged entrance for the players. Examples of non-theatre are Edgbaston, Hove, Southampton and Trent Bridge; the theatrical entrances are at The Parks, Aigburth and Worcester. The chance for perfection has been thrown away in the new facility at the Oval. The batsman starts to make his spectacular entrance from the lofty dressing room only to turn sharply left for the final flight of stairs as if he has had second thoughts and is hoping to get lost in the crowd.

Jonathan Rice has a marvellous eye for the character of the game, as you will see. I just wish he could have seen the original St Helen's pavilion at Swansea – 89 steps down through the ranks of the members: you could imagine the fanfares as you walked out to bat.

On the way back the standing ovation was to be recommended. On the other hand, the silent retreat was agony. Getting out first ball, as it once happened to me – Lewis b Crump 0 – was like ascending to hell.

Tony Lewis

Acknowledgements

Many people have helped in giving Paul and me access to the pavilions featured in this book. In particular, we would like to acknowledge the help given to us by John Baker, Billy Barham, Nigel Bett, Harry Brind, David Butler, Robert Chadwick, Harry Dalling, Mike Fatkin, Peter Foster, John Found, Ray Gilson, David Goodyear, Chris Hassell, Jim Hudson, John Hutchinson, Abe Lincoln, Mark Lucas, Geoff Mercer, Tommy Meneer, John Nelson, Michael Parkinson, Geoff Partridge, Simon Porter, Patrick Scott, Bill Snowden, Robert Speer, Mike Stanger, Lt.-Col. John Stephenson, Chris Taylor, Ken Tucker, David Wedden and Bob Winthrope.

I would also like to thank Tony Lewis, for his help and his foreword, without which this book would have been a couple of pages shorter.

JR

Introduction

CRICKET PAVILIONS, like jockstraps, can be large, medium or small and, like jockstraps, their size is no real gauge of the pleasures that lurk within. They can be brick and concrete, lath and plaster or in some cases cardboard and corrugated iron. They are light and friendly, or dingy and threatening; fully equipped with a bar and historic photographs, or barely sanitary with only a gas boiler and a splintery floor. They stand proudly at the edge of some of the most beautiful landscape in Britain, or hide guiltily beneath the glowering factory chimneys of some Victorian industrialist's ambitions.

The Concise Collins Dictionary defines a pavilion as 'a building at a sports ground, esp. a cricket pitch, in which players change etc.' Its rival publication, the Concise Oxford, adds a further dimension by defining it as a 'light ornamental building, esp. one attached to cricket or other ground for spectators and players.' This schism, so succinctly pinpointed by the two dictionaries, between the building 'in which players change' and the building 'for spectators and players', is the major factor in the development of the architecture and aesthetics of cricket pavilions in Britain. Originally, the pavilion was merely a tent or other such flimsy structure (from the Latin *papilio* – a tent or butterfly) in which people were able to retain their modesty while changing for sporting activity, the inland version of the Victorian bathing machine. We must assume that the players did not invite spectators to watch while they slipped into something more suitable, so the Concise Oxford's conviction that a pavilion these days is for spectators and players (note that the spectators are mentioned before the players) represents a fundamental shift of power away from the performers to their public. It also reflects the damp English climate in which spectators need shelter just as much as the players.

As the twentieth century braces itself for the twenty-first, we are beginning to identify further trends in what the point of a pavilion seems to be. At the top end of the market, where professional cricket attracts money as a drying cowpat attracts flies, the pavilion is turning into an executive entertainment centre with all the relevance to cricket of its sister structure, the Wigmore Street massage parlour. This is of course a direct and inevitable result of the abolition of the distinction between the amateur and the professional in the early 1960s. As soon as the amateur, who used the pavilion as his club, became officially extinct, the players were all treated as professionals and asked to use the back door please. The pavilion became the clubhouse for an exclusively non-playing membership.

We therefore now have three main types of cricket pavilion – the place where cricketers change, the place where cricketers change and spectators watch, and the place where members enjoy a pleasant day despite the occasional interruption to watch the cricket.

Type A is now almost exclusively restricted to the villages of Britain. Rickety sheds, disused stables and rude huts with no hooks, no windows and no electricity are the pride of hundreds of village cricket clubs from Cornwall to Inverness and beyond.

They leak in the rain and they have no locks on the doors but still the vandals break in rather than walk in. They have no loos, although the all-pervading smell suggests otherwise. If they ever build one, it will be a toilet, not a lavatory. The smartest Type A pavilions do have showers, but no soap. Every club has plans to knock them down and build something much better, but they survive, mainly because nobody ever quite gets round to organizing that extra fund-raising jumble sale and charity swim which will make their plans become reality.

Type B, the pavilion for spectators and players, is slowly becoming the mainstay of British club cricket. Once upon a time, when cricket was played on the village green, there was no need to provide food, drink and warmth for the few friends, relations and dogs who came to watch the cricketers, because there was an inn on the green which did all that and more. Indeed, the development of cricket and the siting of pitches in the eighteenth and nineteenth centuries was in many cases decided by where the pub was, so the pavilion was meant to be just a building in which players change. But the twentieth century gave us progress, whether we wanted it or not. The building of roads, the expansion of the population and the rise of the property developer all meant that more and more cricket grounds have been repositioned more than a gentle stroll away from the pub, so the cricketers have had to bring the pub with them to their new home. The way to decide whether a pavilion is a building in which players change or a light ornamental building for spectators and players is to see whether it has a bar. If so, it is Type B; if not, you are in a Type A pavilion.

A Type C pavilion is easily recognizable. It has a doorman who tries hard not to let anybody in. It also has a side door for the players, and no route map from the players' changing rooms to the pitch. David Steele got lost on his way from the changing rooms at Lord's to the wicket to make his debut for England at Lord's in 1975, and Derek Pringle went to the wrong gate to get back into the Oval pavilion after his dismissal for England against Australia fourteen years later. It was not the players' sense of direction which was awry, it is just that the members come first in pavilions like these, and members do not need to know how to get from the changing rooms, which they never use, to the playing area, which they never set foot on. This particular problem does not arise with Type A or Type B pavilions.

Type C pavilions also have bars, offices, television rooms and reading rooms on at least three storeys, and a sightscreen that blocks the view of up to forty per cent of the members eighty per cent of the time. Type C pavilions all are designed to cope with many more spectators than players, so are no longer really pavilions by either of our dictionary definitions at all. They are clubs (usually gentlemen's clubs at that) and grandstands, offices and restaurants. They are treasure troves of cricket nostalgia and have cricket memorabilia on every wall and in every bookcase and cabinet. They can be relics of Victorian monumental architecture at its worst, or Sixties functionalism at its least attractive. They can be beautiful, practical and timeless.

This book is an unstructured stroll around fifty or so cricket pavilions in Britain, chosen for no particular reason except that they were the ones that came to mind when the idea for the book was first put forward. We have missed out many of the largest, smallest, most beautiful and most tumbledown and for this we make no apologies. All cricket pavilions are there because they reflect the national and local passion for cricket, a passion that is expressed equally by the village cricketers content to undress in sub-Oxfam conditions in order to get a game of cricket, and by the club members in the august county pavilions where grown men can be boys again in their devotion to a game which quite possibly they have never played. This book is a tribute to that passion.

Bath: Type A pavilion

Queen Elizabeth School: Type A pavilion

Mullion: Type B pavilion

Truro: Type B pavilion

Abergavenny

·GWENT, SOUTH WALES·

BY ALPHABETICAL accident, my tour of cricket pavilions begins at Abergavenny, but this is as good a place as any to set the standards for the pavilions which follow. For a start, there is the ground itself. Somebody told me before I went there that it was 'perhaps the most beautiful of all the Glamorgan grounds', which is a distinction of minor value when you consider that its competition only includes places like Cardiff and Newport. Abergavenny turned out to be a small but unorthodox ground, almost crying out for the use of the adjective 'quaint'. And the pavilion is worth including in any catalogue of homes of sport.

The Abergavenny pavilion dates from around 1910. The clock on the roof was 'presented by Mr and Mrs Harry Lyons, Abergavenny, April 30th 1921', according to the plaque underneath. It is that rarity among pavilion clocks, one that works. The groundsman, Kenneth Mackenzie (a Gaelic-speaking Scot who seems entirely at home in South Wales), told me that it has never yet been hit by a cricket ball, although many people have tried. 'We've lost a few tiles on the roof, but the clock is still there.'

Inside the pavilion, which is certainly very small by first-class standards, there are all the traditional fixtures and fittings of a Good Pavilion. The main room features a board listing the names of all captains and chairmen through the years. There is a one-armed bandit there, too, and a plaque on the wall above the bar next to a hideous plastic Leicester Building Society clock, which reads, 'Presented by Muriel Laycock in memory of her father Vern Jones, July 1964.' This has nothing to do with

the clock, but comes from a wooden bench which has failed to survive. This is not the only example of misplaced information in the pavilions of Britain.

The pavilion was originally just what is now the main room, but it is an invariable law of pavilions that they grow with time, like children's feet. The section in which the changing rooms are now located was built on to the back of the pavilion at some later stage. The pitch is not visible from either changing room, so the players tend to sit in the main room or on the benches outside while waiting their turn to bat.

The South Wing is new. It was built in the Seventies and is an upmarket saloon bar – parquet flooring, little round tables and no beer stains on the walls. Instead there is an impressive array of tour pennants above the bar. I am not sure of the relevance of the 'Worcester Police C.C. Australia '89' pennant, but at least it adds a touch of Australiana to what is otherwise a very British pavilion.

It is also obviously a Welsh pavilion. There is even a little notice on the wall pointing out that 'this facility was provided with the aid of a grant from the Sports Council of Wales. Cyngor Chwaraeon Cymru.' Like all other Welsh pavilions, it has an excellent kitchen, with two microwaves, two electric cookers, a chest freezer, a fridge and the ubiquitous water boiler.

The only typically Welsh accessory that is not to be found at Abergavenny is a piano. All other pavilions in the Land of Song have a piano.

Aigburth

·LIVERPOOL CRICKET CLUB, AIGBURTH, MERSEYSIDE·

LANCASHIRE COUNTY Cricket Club plays once a year at Aigburth on the southern edge of Liverpool, eager to enjoy the delights of a pavilion that is a far grander building than a mere league side needs. That Liverpool Cricket Club is a league club rather than a county club is proved by the Availability notice on the main board: I have yet to discover a county club which has to ask the players to let them know on which days they will be available. No county player's availability is in doubt, because county cricketers do not take their summer holidays in the summer; nor do they stay at home to mow the lawn on a Saturday afternoon. At Liverpool, they live with these problems like any village club.

The Aigburth pavilion is what makes Liverpool CC different from any village club. Aigburth is a hive of surprises. It was designed on the grand scale and still reflects that oddly attractive self-important grandeur which typifies all that is best and worst in Victoriana. The two main club rooms are called the Chavasse Room and the Dougall Room, after two First World War VCs. Capt. Noel Chavasse was a VC and bar, so his room is the grander of the two. It has an old tiled fireplace in one corner, ceiling fans combined with turn-of-the-century light fittings overhead, Burtonwood Bitter beer mats on all tables and mantelpieces, and the board listing club presidents and captains since the ground was opened in 1881. The Chavasse Room also has a fruit machine flickering quietly but incessantly, a robotic icon of 1990s culture trapped in a Victorian time warp.

Lt. Eric Dougall only won one VC, so his memorial room is less sumptuous. It is behind the Chavasse Room, and unless there happens to be a bit of action at deep fine leg, no cricket can be seen. It is carpeted as completely as the Chavasse Room, however, and contains the trophy cabinet. 'This cabinet is alarmed 24 hours a day. Please do not touch.' Without such a dire warning, how could a light-fingered trophy hunter resist the Newton-Le-Willows Sports Club Burtonwood Shield (1989 winners MHAC Ladies), the LCC IntraSection Quiz Winners Cup, or the Arthur Fox Trophy 1975? I had to make a conscious effort to keep my hands in my pockets.

Lt. Dougall was certainly a Liverpool man, and would therefore have been quite relaxed about the presence of a jukebox in his room. He might be rather more upset by the choice of music on the jukebox – plenty of Madonna and Kylie Minogue, two records by Pat Boone, several Elvis hits and more by Buddy Holly and Chuck Berry, but no Beatles. There is even one Rolling Stones single in there, but the only Liverpool artist represented on the jukebox was Liverpool and England winger John Barnes, whose contribution to the England World Cup squad's chart-topping hit of those World Cup days of 1990 will, unfortunately, never be forgotten.

On the ground floor is a large photograph of W. G. Grace, a snooker room and the Taverners Bar, but for those whose bodies cannot take further deterioration, there is also the best equipped gym I have seen in any pavilion anywhere. Aigburth is indeed a hive of surprises.

Ambleside

·CUMBRIA·

EVERYBODY KNOWS that for outstanding natural beauty, you either watch the collected *oeuvre* of Ingrid Bergman or else you go to the Lake District. But even by the standards of that region (the Lake District, not any part of Miss Bergman), the setting of Ambleside Cricket Club's ground is breathtaking. It is a little shelf on the hillside, fenced off from the sheep in the fields surrounding. Dry stone walls criss-cross the peaks beyond Rydal and even in the parched summer of 1990 the grass is a deep reassuring English green.

It would be stretching things to say that the Ambleside pavilion lives up to its surroundings, but at least it has the good sense to be invisible from the road. It is a cement-coloured Snowcem blockhouse on a brick base with a peeling black painted headband running below the flat bitumen roof – another strictly utilitarian piece of architecture. A board on the outside of the pavilion says 'Today's Sponsors', but the space for the sponsors' name is blank.

Inside the pavilion, the true nature of Ambleside CC is apparent. Tea has just finished, and the clearing up is waiting to be done. I helped by eating a leftover slice of a particularly good orange jelly gâteau, but the five wives among the chaos seemed unconcerned. Their minds were on other things.

Between them, they were nursing, changing or just holding six children under the age of three. One little boy was asleep on the floor using a cricket bat as a pillow. The baby boom is alive and well in Ambleside. 'Shows how much effort our husbands put into their cricket,' said one of the ladies, looking remarkably cheerful under the circumstances.

Ambleside are in the Fifth Division of their league, but are, I was loyally assured, working their way up. The pavilion is rather better than Fifth Division, but could do with a little working up itself. For the past few years they have been meaning to redecorate when the season ends, as a bare patch of wall in the corner testifies, but for some reason they have not quite got round to it yet. The pavilion is a structure of the 1960s, well remembered by the Ambleside wives as somewhere they used to come as children. 'And they've still got the same lampshades,' a remark that caused a great deal of mirth, which is surprising for such unexciting little lampshades, hanging like flypaper from the ceiling.

On the bar are the team photographs, mainly unframed. I assume their presence on the bar rather than on the wall is part of the Great Redecoration Scheme, which may also involve the creation of a trophy cabinet. I hope it does, because Ambleside have the most eclectic selection of pots I have found anywhere on my travels. They have a pennant from Randwick Wanderers Cricket Club British Isles Tour 1978, and a matching Norman O'Neill autograph bat, signed by all the Randwick players and a few more besides. They have a huge cup inscribed 'Tartan Keg Trophy for Annual Competition', but what annual competition it was, or when, is not disclosed. Any connection with cricket is purely coincidental. The final trophy is for 'Most Humorous Tableau In The Ambleside Festival', a prize they picked up in 1977. I'm surprised they've only won it that once.

Ampton

·AMPTON AND CULFORD CRICKET CLUB, BURY ST EDMUNDS, SUFFOLK·

GETTING TO Ampton and Culford's ground is no simple matter, but the pavilion is well worth all the navigational stress. It is an astonishing place, described by one writer as 'the Lord's of East Anglia'. Actually it looks nothing like Lord's, but what he means is that Ampton, like Headquarters, is one architect's way of defining the splendours of cricket. It was built in 1902, or perhaps 1903, entirely of wood. Its crowning glory is a massive thatched roof, and as you approach the ground from behind the pavilion, it resembles nothing so much as an Australian stockade or an Arizona corral of a century ago. One almost expects Ned Kelly or Billy the Kid to be holed up in the kitchen as the forces of the law close in. I went nervously inside to check, but the most menacing item in the kitchen turned out to be the instructions for brewing the tea. They looked almost as lethal as a bullet from an outlaw's revolver: '14 teabags for the first pot – fill to top. 2 more to top up.'

The long room at Ampton is not a room at all, but merely an open-fronted covered area, some fifteen yards wide by six yards deep, with a pitted and splintery floor on a brick-built base some three feet above pitch level. The front of the pavilion, facing south towards the pitch, is entirely open, supported by six elderly wooden pillars against which generations of woodworm have conducted regular assaults. In Edwardian times the batsmen must have enjoyed the almost melodramatic impression they would have made on the parasol-toting young ladies of the parish who stood in admiration around the boundary; as their heroes crossed the floor and stepped lightly but resolutely into the playing area, bat under arm, multi-coloured cap at a jaunty angle and those funny green spiky gloves ready to be pulled on during the march to the wicket. Even today, the pavilion looks so much like the stage of some provincial repertory company that it would seem more natural for the fielding side to be the spectators and the players in the pavilion to be the central focus of action. One almost expects to hear at any minute from stage right the mild-mannered friend of the hero asking politely, 'Anyone for cricket?'

There are no trophies, photographs or signed cricket bats tracing the history of the club, just an awe-inspiring pavilion with ninety years of stud-marks on the floor and muddy football imprints of more recent vintage on the walls. I expect they tell the casual visitor more about the spirit of the club than any amount of framed scorecards or Balls With Which Our Opening Bowler Took 9 Wickets Against The Other Lot which infest most other and lesser pavilions.

When the sun shines at Ampton, it is easy to forget the twentieth century ever happened. 'Where, indeed,' asked one over-romantic village cricketer shortly after the Second World War, 'among the pavilions of Heaven do wild bees, as here, store their honeycombs beneath the timbers? If Heaven's pavilions enthrone the game so magnificently as this, cricketers must early in their Elysian innings forget their heyday on earth.' That is the secret of Ampton. Even a duck, three dropped catches and a two-hour stint of umpiring can seem like a cricketing heyday.

Arundel

·ARUNDEL CASTLE, SUSSEX·

'THIS GROUND was made by Henry 15 Duke of Norfolk 1895. This pavilion was built by his son and was opened by S. C. Griffith, D.F.C., T.D., Sussex and England, President of the Martlets, Secretary of the M.C.C., 27 June 1965.' The notice just inside the main door proudly announces the pavilion's pedigree. Arundel is now recognized not only as one of the loveliest grounds in Britain, with Arundel Castle nestling on its south-eastern edge, but also as one with a wicket good enough for first-class cricket.

What I like most about the pavilion is the roof. The small deep russet tiles give the building an air of solidity and gravitas which normally only comes with age. What I like least about the pavilion is the hot water system. Arundel achieves what most smaller pavilions cannot: a constant flow of hot water from the showers, at a temperature entirely unaffected by what is going on in the next shower, the wash basins or the other elegant pieces of plumbing dotted liberally around the building. The only slight difficulty is that this constant temperature is around 70° Celsius, which causes third-degree burns in those cricketers foolhardy enough to spend more than a couple of milliseconds under the shower. A large procession of smelly but only slightly scalded cricketers emerged from the shower area the day I played there.

The Long Room is clean and almost ostentatiously underfurnished. It contains the statutory portrait of W. G. Grace, who scored 1,000 runs in the May of the year the Arundel ground was made, but far more originality is shown in the exhibit on the opposite wall. A painting by Ray Perry of *Cricket at Arundel* is flanked by two framed poems, one by Peter Wood dated 3 August 1936, and another by Reggie Winn. The painting displays more artistic skill than either of the poems, although I like Peter Wood's opening quatrain:

> Beneath the stately Dukely trees
> His Grace's peasants on their knees
> Were praying that his Grace might not
> Be beaten by the first he got.

There are other pictures around the walls: two cartoons lampooning the late Duke's love of cricket, and a portrait in oils of the Duke in whites with a bat under his arm striding out to (or perhaps, beaten by the first he got, back from) the wicket. There is a bar, well propped up by non-playing members wearing the Arundel Castle CC tie, and signs all around stating, 'No studs or spikes in cricket school', which naturally leads a top investigative journalist like me to look for the cricket school. To be honest, it is not that hard to find. It is along a corridor decorated with Lillywhite coaching prints from 1860 – 'No. 1, Standing In Attitude', 'No. 2, The Draw' – but the school itself is definitely late twentieth century. Lucky indeed are the young cricketers of Arundel and its surrounds who have the chance to improve their game in such perfect conditions (even without studs or spikes).

The people who just play and watch here are pretty lucky too.

Baldon Green

·OXFORDSHIRE·

THE HOME of the South Oxon Farmers Cricket Club is Baldon Green. The ground is one of the most classically rustic in England, with thatched cottages all around, and the village pub, the Seven Stars, set deep on the southernmost edge. So simple is its beauty that it was no surprise to find an amateur watercolourist painting a view of the houses beyond the lush green grass of the outfield. However, it was also no surprise that she was painting with her back to the Baldon Green pavilion, which is the only eyesore in the neighbourhood. Fortunately, it is a tiny eyesore, no more than thirty feet wide and twenty-five feet deep, built of brick and wood on the north-western edge of the playing area, but all the same it is an anomaly which ranks firmly in the carbuncle class for architectural merit.

Two things distinguish every match against the South Oxon Farmers. The first is that the main road through the village actually runs through the playing area, separating the pavilion from the square. Batting is, of course, far less dangerous than fielding, as once across the road, the batsman does not have to watch out for traffic until the end of his innings a few minutes later. The fielders have to follow the Green Cross code every time the ball is hit towards the pavilion, and many an extra run has been scored thanks to the timely arrival of a car travelling sedately from mid-wicket to deep fine leg. The alternative is to place a fielder permanently on the pavilion side of the road, but that is to leave him open to the temptations of the second distinguishing feature of games on Baldon Green – the teas.

It is quite astonishing that a pavilion as unprepossessing as this one should regularly be the source of such wonderful teas. To produce anything free of BSE and listeria from its confines seems a minor miracle, to say nothing of the meringues, cakes and seventeen shades of sandwich which are routinely served to hungry cricketers half-way through the afternoon. The tea is served on trestle tables outside the pavilion so backward square legs or deep extra covers patrolling the edge of the ground nearest the pavilion immediately before tea are often distracted by the feast unfurling before them, which can have a negative effect on their fielding skills. After tea, nobody moves for about half an hour.

The pavilion is one room with pegs fixed fitfully around its walls, the sunlight seeping through small windows with wire mesh over them to prevent breakages. The only piece of furniture in the pavilion is a large white chest bearing the legend, 'Seven Stars Angling Club, Oxford'. In the beams supporting the roof are stored tent poles and guy-ropes, presumably for use when the pavilion finally collapses under the combined pressures of dry rot, death watch beetle and outraged connoisseurs of architecture.

Outside there is also a bench, 'Presented by members of S. Oxon Farmers Cricket Club in memory of Dennis Walker, 1953'. Hidden behind the pavilion, in an undergrowth of nettles and brambles, is the gents' urinal, a combination of breeze-blocks and a farmyard smell that adds its own subtle nuances to the character of the pavilion.

But it is worth it all for the teas.

Barham
·KENT·

IN DECEMBER 1945 a letter went out to all parishioners of Barham, in which they were told that 'it has been decided in memory of the eleven young men of this Parish who have made the supreme sacrifice in the World War 1939–45 . . . to purchase and lay out a Sports and Recreation Ground'. They also proposed 'to erect a pavillion [sic] on the front of which will be placed a Memorial Tablet'.

Thus was set in motion the chain of events which led, rather slowly, to the opening of the new sports pavilion at Barham Memorial Playing Fields almost seven years later, at the Annual Fete and Sports on 28 June 1952. It was presided over by Tom Arter, the Chairman of the Committee who 'throughout, had done all he could and had cheered them on when they got downhearted', according to the guest of honour, the Chairman of Bride-Blean rural district council. (Forty years on, Mr Arter still takes a close interest in the club and the pavilion. He is the custodian of the keys to the place.) The Rector, Mr Hare, then read out the names of the twenty-four who fell in the 1914–1918 war (including Lord Kitchener, a local landowner) and of the eleven who died in the Second World War, whose names are still recorded on a plaque in the pavilion. There are many other pavilions, from Lord's to Bournville, which record the names of members who died in battle, but no other that I have found which was built specifically to be their memorial.

If the memorial is in the quality of the architecture, then it hardly justified the sacrifice. It is built solidly, as only post-war prefabs can be, on the same general lines as a corporation bus shelter. It is not beautiful. From the outside, there is no indication that it serves as a memorial to anybody. Only the newly-painted sign over the main entrance, boldly stating 'Barham C.C. Founded 1833', gives any indication at all of its use. In 1990, large wooden shutters were added and then painted an interesting rust colour, partly to keep out vandals but more particularly to keep out the winds which were wont to come in under the eaves and lift the roof off on a blustery day. Keeping out the vandals was for many years a lost cause too, as the messages carved on the walls indicate: 'Anita + Martin Cool' and 'Anita 4 Posty' are scratched on consecutive bricks, only a few inches away from 'LA loves AR'. If AR is Anita again, we know where she spends her Saturday nights. I wonder if LA knows about Posty, and what makes Martin so cool.

The visitor's changing room is not the most comfortable I have ever used, but it is not because the Barham club is inhospitable or unfriendly. The home changing room is just as bad. A notice on the wall, and repeated on the back of the door, says that teas cost £17, 'which includes £5 towards the cost of food at the Palm Tree on the Elham Valley road.' Never arrange to rush away from the ground after playing at Barham: always enjoy the hospitality at the Palm Tree. The same notice also notes the playing hours (30 minutes maximum for tea) and adds, 'We will try to keep up an over rate of 20 overs an hour.' Clearly they have never played the West Indians here. It matters not who won or lost at Barham, but how we play the game. Maybe it's not such an ugly memorial after all.

Bath

·CITY OF BATH RECREATION GROUND AND BATH CRICKET CLUB·

THE CITY of Bath Recreation Ground is a large open area, the eastern end of which houses Bath Rugby Football Club, while at the southern edge stands the pavilion which acts as home base whenever Somerset County Cricket Club plays at Bath. The entire northern side of the Recreation Ground is enclosed by the Bath Magistrates Courts, which are sturdy and architecturally unstimulating. The same adjectives could be applied to the cricket pavilion opposite. When Somerset play here, the pavilion is camouflaged by bright marquees and rows of gaudy plastic seats and the whole ground is a blaze of civic colour. When nobody is playing here, the pavilion is a bleak outpost.

It is built of wood, painted dark brown, and the lino on the floor reinforces the sturdiness and practicality. The roof is newly tiled with an elegant bell tower on top, which in turn is capped by an elegant lightning conductor and an elegant weather-vane. The bell in the bell tower works well: tethered to a hook by the bar inside is a rope which, when pulled, causes the bell to ring out in a desolate peal across the Recreation Ground as though warning of escaped prisoners from the Magistrates Court. There are also alarm bells all over the pavilion, despite the fact that security seems extraordinarily lax. The day I visited Bath, there was no game and nobody working on the pitch, but the pavilion door was wide open.

The lack of security may be connected to the lack of items worth stealing. There are no trophies and no cash registers, just a dog-eared notice on the gents' changing-room wall with details of various Peter Roebuck Benefit Nights, with a request for volunteers to attend them. The home team uses the gents' facilities, it seems. The ladies' changing-room, which I assume is also used by visiting cricket teams, adjoins the only ladies' lavatory in Britain containing three urinals. The main room has three fire extinguishers, a place for a dartboard (the board has been stored elsewhere); and a gas oven of sufficient age to justify the presence of those three fire extinguishers.

Across the road, only six runs away for the best of Somerset's big hitters, is the private Bath Cricket Club (see page 11). Their clubhouse is smart, modern and efficient, so it is odd that the scorebox in the far corner of the ground should be so comparatively dilapidated. The flowers in front of the clubhouse are better tended than any I have seen in England, and they possess a bowling machine for net practice. But there are broken tiles on the roof of the scorebox to contrast with the pristine roof at the Recreation Ground, and inside deck-chairs, matting and plastic hoses are piled high in a jumble of partly used accessories. Yet the scoreboard is electric. It is not as advanced as the unreadable item at Lord's, but it is technologically well ahead of anything I have seen at a club or school ground.

That two such grounds should exist so close to each other is a tribute to the interest in cricket in this ancient city. That the private club should be smaller and less well pavilioned than the council-owned one is a political contradiction after a decade of Thatcherism, but who cares? Everybody knows cricket and politics do not mix.

Bournville

·BIRMINGHAM, WARWICKSHIRE·

I SUPPOSE I should have expected it. After all, Cadbury Schweppes owns Bournville Cricket Club. All the same, I was not ready for that moment when I parked the car next to the pavilion and stepped out into the fresh air. An overwhelming smell of chocolate enshrouded me. There are many smells which remind me of cricket pavilions: the pungency of linseed oil, the freshness of a new lick of paint or creosote in the spring, the inescapable tang of tuna fish sandwiches or the even less subtle body odours of a home dressing room; but only at Bournville is the smell an overpowering one of Dairy Milk Chocolate and Creme Eggs. The new Creme Egg factory, I was reliably informed, is on the third floor of one of the buildings in the factory complex overlooking the ground. A big six could bring production to a halt.

After the smell comes a sensation of colour. The pavilion is painted chocolate and white and green, like a jumbled stack of Milky Bars in a forest. Part of the outside has recently been beautifully restored. 'They stripped it all out,' I was told. 'It is good to see proper carpentry and proper joiners at work.' From an architectural point of view, I am sure the work was well worth it. But as a home for a cricket club, Bournville's pavilion is sadly over-large and under-used.

It is three storeys high. The top floor is a gymnasium with enormous high ceilings, wall bars for the keep-fit fanatics and pale green walls to camouflage those feeling ill from over-exertion. The back stairs are like any other pavilion's hidden parts — a Sargasso Sea of cast-off sporting equipment and empty drinks cans — but the gymnasium itself is spotless. At the back of the building, clearly visible to passers-by on the pavement, is a notice which states positively that 'Pigeon shooting, horse riding, coursing, dog racing and any game in which there is competition for monetary prizes are strictly prohibited. No intoxicating liquors shall be sold, bought or consumed on the grounds.' The lines of the pavilion look a little more severe now. It is a shell without the crab, a perfect home which needs somebody living there.

There is a tea-room, a bar (but no licence, of course), and a notice-board that lists the names of those who owe the club money for cricket sweaters. It also proclaims Bournville's results in Division One of the Home Brewery Midland Counties League, in which they prosper despite their founder's strict teetotalism. There is a large wrought copper memorial to Our Glorious Dead of the two wars listing an astonishingly savage total of 141 names. A wreath was still there when I visited seven months after Remembrance Sunday. There is a dispensing machine on the wall, which at Bournville does not dispense cigarettes or condoms, but four kinds of chocolate.

Bournville is a beautiful building but a dull pavilion. All the club photographs and trophies are stored two hundred yards down the road at the Bournville Club, which is the social hub of the company. If you separate the club from the cricket, you get a place like Bournville, a pavilion which is all packaging and no contents. Cadbury's customers would complain if their Creme Eggs were like that.

Bovey Tracey and Shobrooke Park

·BOVEY TRACEY CRICKET CLUB AND SHOBROOKE PARK CRICKET CLUB·

BOVEY TRACEY Cricket Club has played at the Recreation Ground, Newton Road, since 1852, when they were able to take over a large building which probably began life as a barn, and which has been their home ever since. The legend, 'B.T.C.C. 1852', which dominates the front of the building, establishes its pedigree for all visitors. Cricket has been played at Shobrooke Park, about twenty miles away just the other side of Exeter, since 1890, although the sign on the scoreboard attached to their pavilion is more diffident about its age. 'S.P.C.C. Formed 18 ' is all it says, and it requires sharper eyes to notice the date 1890 over the door.

At Bovey Tracey, the kitchen may not be enormous, but it is clean, efficient and well stocked. At Shobrooke Park, the kitchen contains a Calor gas powered tea-urn, two flagons of orange juice, a Clarendon Nomads 1978 tour pennant, a jar of teabags and a heavily amended tea ladies' rota. From it I learned that Jackie did teas for Ottery St Mary on 29 April. Beryl and Tricia did for the Gentlemen of Old Windsor on 4 July, while Mandy refreshed the Worthing Foresters on 17 July. The young men of Trinity College Cambridge on 27 June feasted upon the culinary delights of Steve, who may or may not be a tea lady, but the Shobrooke players know the reputation of Trinity men from of old.

The Bovey Tracey pavilion roof went up in smoke well over a century ago, so the upper part of the pavilion is newer than the rest. It is difficult to arrange a fire that does not destroy the roof rather more completely than the rest of the building, which is

probably why no tried and trusted arsonist has been let loose at Shobrooke Park, whose saving grace is its wonderful thatched roof. If it were to happen, the pavilion might contain delights equal to the Bovey Tracey scorebox. The scorers' view of the cricket at Bovey Tracey is probably even better than the umpires', being directly behind and above the bowler's arm, but all the same I do not envy the scorers their job. After all, they have to cope with the Devon Cricket League Points Scoring System, which is explained, clearly enough for anybody with a Nobel Prize in Physics to understand, on a notice pinned up on the wall. One of the less complicated clauses states that 'One point is scored by *winning* side batting second for every two wickets standing at end of game, provided that total batting points awarded under (1A) + (2B) does not exceed 5.' Of course, how silly of me not to realize that.

At Shobrooke Park (see page 2), virtually the only thing dangling from the walls is the paint. There is one framed photograph in the tea-room bearing the hand-written message 'presented by John Roach', and the visitors' changing-room has a mirror for very thin people. But there is nothing as up-market as original Jack Russell cartoons signed by members of the Gloucestershire county side or the 'Umpires Five Minute Bell' which Bovey Tracey boasts. At Shobrooke Park the Canada Geese fly over the pavilion every evening around six o'clock. The view they have, of the roof and the cedar-lined ground, is the best available. At Bovey Tracey, those same geese would need to come inside to see the pavilion at its best.

Bramham

·NEAR LEEDS, YORKSHIRE·

BRAMHAM CRICKET Club's pavilion is easily visible from the A1. When a cricket match is in progress, the traffic provides a continuous movement behind the bowler's arm, but most drivers scything through the traffic north of Leeds do not bother to stop and take a closer interest. This is a pity, because Bramham's pavilion has a unique history. It is, as far as I have been able to find out, the only cricket pavilion in Britain which began life as a troop dormitory in Pocklington.

Bramham's cricket ground and pavilion are owned by the Bayford Energy Company, whose offices are a clump of trees away. Bramham Cricket Club have rented the ground for six years since they moved from Bramham Park, and thanks to the cut and thrust of big city takeovers, Bayfords are already their third landlord in that time. For reasons that I was not fully able to understand, Bramham only rent half the pavilion from Bayfords, and the half they rent does not include the front door. However, they do not seem to be obliged to climb in and out of a window in the Bramham half of the pavilion every time they play at home, so we can assume that Bayfords turn a blind eye to their trespassing. The half they do rent includes the kitchen, and it is also the part which is marginally better decorated. Pavilions which are there for the use of the players more than the spectators (and not just because they usually outnumber the spectators: that happens often enough at county matches too) tend not to be particularly well appointed, and Bramham is no exception. Their half has a bedraggled green carpet on the floor and a Hoover and a space heater stored in a corner, signs of a

little pride of ownership, but very little else. There is a notice-board on the wall outside the home dressing-room which features the first eleven averages for the season so far. They do not make pleasant reading in a season in which Bramham were faced with relegation to Division Three of the Wetherby League, but no doubt the opposition were much cheered by them. The club trophies, team photos and sundry memorabilia are in the local pub. The Bayfords half has the tables and chairs. The Bramham half has the kitchen and the changing-rooms, but the Bayfords half has the table tennis table. The toilets are outside. The ladies' is a chemical affair of minimal comfort, and the gents' is a corrugated iron shed. I doubt whether either party claims proprietary rights over them.

There are one or two signs of luxury that show that, given a chance, the Bramham pavilion might be as splendid as Lord's. The dressing-room sinks are both equipped with bars of Imperial Leather soap rather than institutional carbolic, and there were green, orange and purple paper chains dangling from the ceiling in the aftermath of the evening in which they entertained their regular tourists from Brandon in County Durham to what the Bramham team described as 'a barbecue and a few beers'. I was told that Brandon has a smart new pavilion, and the slight overtones of envy in the voice were unmistakable. Still, even a half share in what once was a military dormitory just off the A1 is better than nothing, and if the choice has to be made between a thriving club like Bramham or a beautiful pavilion like Bournville, most cricketers would head for Bramham.

Bridgetown

·BRIDGETOWN CRICKET CLUB, SOMERSET·

SOME CRICKET grounds are hard to reach, and seem barely worth the effort when you get there. Some deliberately hide themselves away, so that nobody but the most knowledgeable of local inhabitants knows where they are (I speak feelingly of Cheltenham and Scarborough in this context), and others are on show to even the most casual of passers-by. Bridgetown is certainly hard to reach – getting there from any distance is a major achievement of navigation and perseverance in the summer holiday traffic – but once you are in Bridgetown, there is no possibility that you will not find the ground.

Bridgetown is not a big place, but cricket seems to be central to their lives. The town is dotted with houses with names like 'The Wickets', 'Bat and Ball' and, probably, 'Dunbowlin'. The ground is on a small patch of level ground between a bend in the A396 as it flanks the River Exe and the edge of Exmoor, and to get to the ground you have to park your car by the roadside and cross the river by means of a very rickety wooden bridge. It is a hair-raising experience at the best of times, but if the pavilion had a bar, the life expectancy of cricketers on a moonless evening after the match would be minimal. Fortunately, there is no bar: the Badgers Holt pub is a hundred yards up the road.

'B.C.C. 1924' says the shield above the pavilion door. Not even 66 years of cricket have kept the pheasants from pottering around the outfield or the ducks from the river. The sounds I associate with Bridgetown are not the gentle thwack of willow upon leather but the rural sound effects of ducks quacking, pheasants nibbling and, above all, sheep bleating. If moles made noises, they would add to nature's cacophony as there is clear evidence of our velvet-coated friends in the outfield. The ground is fenced and stiled, but that does not keep the local ecology at bay.

From the front, the pavilion is one of the most picturesque in Britain. The thatched roof, the oak panelling and oak benches and the sweep of the hillside behind all give Bridgetown's pavilion a deserved high rating among landscape painters and photographers. Inside, it is still highly picturesque, although whether picturesqueness is what active cricketers look for first inside a pavilion is open to discussion. What they usually look for first is the changing room, and this is easy to find at Bridgetown as it bears the legend 'Players Only' above the door. A few hooks on the wall and a mirror are the main fixtures and fittings. The light seeps through the gap between wall and roof, and the space up to the crown of the thatch gives the changing-rooms a deceptive feeling of roominess.

Roominess is most certainly not part of the ambience of the Bridgetown toilet facilities. There are many fairly basic gents' loos around the cricket grounds of Britain, but Bridgetown boasts the only real Australian-style outside dunny that I have stumbled across in my travels. It is hidden behind a hedge behind the pavilion and is no bigger than a Buckingham Palace sentry box, but far less comfortable. Unlike Bridgetown itself, it is easy to reach, but pretty horrible when you get there. But I suppose it is not officially part of Bridgetown pavilion, so it is allowed not to be picturesque.

Canterbury

·THE STUART CHIESMAN PAVILION, KENT COUNTY CRICKET CLUB ST LAWRENCE GROUND, CANTERBURY, KENT·

THE FIRST game at the St Lawrence ground on the south-eastern edge of Canterbury was played in 1847. Ten years later the first permanent structure at the ground was built to provide covered accommodation for spectators, in keeping with the Collins definition of a pavilion, but during fifty years of county cricket at Canterbury the players changed in tents, thus keeping faith with the etymological derivation of the word 'pavilion' into the twentieth century. It was obvious, though, that a county headquarters could not continue indefinitely without permanent changing rooms or a members' bar, and in 1900 the pavilion was completed.

In 1970, it was redeveloped, enlarged and renamed The Stuart Chiesman Pavilion, in honour of the man who was Chairman of Kent CCC from 1959 until he died in 1969. The pavilion is thus a 1970 structure on a 1900 framework.

But beauty is not skin deep, nor even two layers of dark brown brick deep. The interior of the Stuart Chiesman Pavilion may now be little used on match days except as a bar, partly because of the extensive pale blue sightscreens which blot out both sun and cricket, but it is still a friendly place, the headquarters of an informal county club. Things have changed since the despotic Lord Harris dominated the early years of the club, although his portrait still hangs on the wall. It is not alone. As in so many pavilions, portraits hang on every wall. Indeed, the Chiesman Pavilion contains photographs of every capped player in the history of the club, 168 in all, from Lord

Harris and F. A. Mackinnon, the Mackinnon of Mackinnon, in 1882, to Matthew Fleming in 1990. Among them is a portrait of W. G. Grace, who played one game for Kent in 1877 without winning his county cap, and the well-known painting by Chevallier Tayler showing Colin Blythe bowling to J. T. Tyldesley in the 1907 Kent v Lancashire match.

The Chiesman Pavilion also has a case full of relics, of course. It includes Lord Harris's first county cap, embroidered by his mother the Dowager Lady Harris. It contains Fuller Pilch's pads (which he wore underneath his trousers), as well as his snuff box and his wine jug. The ball with which C. J. Burnup skittled the 1899 Australians is there, along with a plate celebrating Colin Cowdrey's hundred centuries and the wallet Colin Blythe was carrying when he was killed in the First World War. The bullet hole goes right through the leather, and through the picture of his mother he always carried with him.

The climb to the upper storey of the pavilion involves negotiating a steep iron staircase which clings to the outside wall, but it is all worth it for the lofty view of the cricket, which is the best in the ground. From there you can see, during Canterbury Cricket Week, the marquees erected for the High Sheriff, the Mayor of Canterbury, the President of Kent CCC and many other dignitaries. Players no longer change in the tents, but spectators enjoy the food and the cricket, and the flags flicker in the breeze like colours at a medieval tournament. Lord Harris and Colin Blythe would still recognize the place.

Cheltenham

·THE COLLEGE GROUND, CHELTENHAM, GLOUCESTERSHIRE·

CHELTENHAM AND Scarborough town councils both obviously feel the same way about motorists, viz. that they should be discouraged from attending cricket festivals. In Scarborough, the RAC signs lead the unwary driver unerringly through a web of not quite straight roads with promises of 'CRICKET', until just as the goal seems to be in sight, all cars are directed into the swimming pool car park. In Cheltenham, they are even more cunning. If you approach the town from the north, you will see, strung out across the road, a large and fully informative banner which proclaims the Cricket Festival. But after that encouraging start, there is nothing else whatsoever to guide the intrepid potential spectator to the ground. After four laps of the centre of Cheltenham, we finally decided to follow the Irish dictum that if you want to go there, I wouldn't start from here, and started again from somewhere else. Plan B worked, but we had reckoned without the final discouragement: the College car-park was full. By the time we settled down to watch Gloucestershire and Surrey locked in championship combat, some of the fun seemed to have gone out of the day.

Cheltenham College is a Victorian public school, and Gloucestershire have played here since 1872. The college pavilion is simply the western end of a large twin-spired school building, which contains the gymnasium, and the other end of which is a rackets court. It is an austere building, with sharp angles, a brooding slate-grey roof and seven large arch windows fronting the pavilion. Above these coffin-shaped windows is a round window in the gable, with a Star of David pattern framing the glass. The building is not inelegant, yet nor is it warm and friendly. Inside, this impression is reinforced. Honest, worthy, clean and dull are the adjectives which leap to mind. The whole ground – the festival marquees, ice-cream vans and second-hand cricketana tents and all – seems to be holding back on the party spirit which is much more obvious at places like Canterbury and Scarborough.

The photographs on the walls of the pavilion long room are a curious mixture of school and county memorabilia. There is a photograph of the Cambridge undergraduate K. S. Duleepsinhji, an old boy of Cheltenham College, standing in front of the scoreboard which shows his record 254 not out against Middlesex in 1927, the highest score ever made at Fenner's. There are many photographs of earlier Cheltenham festivals, pennants from St George's College and The British Schools Montevideo among others, and even a rather odd drawing of Lord's in 1966. There are many rugby football items, too, including a shield confirming that the College side were runners-up in the 1989 Rosslyn Park School Sevens. Yet, as far as I could see, there were no portraits of W. G. Grace in one of the few places where he played regularly.

'NO ADMITTANCE. Cheltenham College Staff, Players and Officials, Severn Sound, Cotswold Hospital Radio ONLY', says a sign on one door into the pavilion. I suggest we leave them to it, and establish ourselves in the makeshift stand on the sunny side of the ground, where we can enjoy the cricket and its imposing setting to the full.

Chislehurst

·CHISLEHURST AND WEST KENT CRICKET CLUB
CHISLEHURST COMMON, KENT·

CRICKET HAS been played on Chislehurst Common since 1738. The Bye-Laws of Chislehurst Common, dated this 16th day of November, 1901, state that 'no person shall play at cricket or any other game . . . except at such times as the conservators may from time to time prescribe', which these days seems to mean three matches a week, on Wednesdays, Saturdays and Sundays, and lacrosse in the winter. Chislehurst and West Kent Cricket Club (why do so many cricket clubs like to be an amalgam of two places at once?) play in the Colmore Kent Metropolitan Cricket League, with mixed success. 'They are a good social club,' I was told, 'but not such a good cricket club.' Sounds like a crowd of cricketers after my own heart.

The pavilion certainly is not 250 years old. The oldest photograph on display inside shows the 1913 team, and the pavilion features in that shot. However, the pervasive influence of the urban vandal of the 1990s makes the pavilion look older than it really is. Looking around at the carefully manicured gardens and the discreet luxury of the surrounding houses, it is hard to imagine this end of Chislehurst as a breeding ground for wanton destruction, but the state of the pavilion cannot be attributed merely to lack of care or lack of funds.

The pavilion looks distinctly shaky. Inside the main room, the social power of the club is evident. The bar, which provides most of the money the club makes, is the only smart part of the room. The clock has stopped at 28 minutes to eight, but although it is not working, at least it exists. A clock which used to hang proudly outside over the main entrance, and which is a feature of many of the old team photographs around the walls, is long gone. Hanging up by the bar, there is a very burnt cricket bat, but no indication as to how it got burnt or why it is worthy of being considered a trophy. One can distinguish that it is a Ken Barrington autograph, so it is of no great age and certainly was not used by or against the ubiquitous Dr W. G. Grace, who spent his final years not far from here, at Eltham. There is also, on the wall between the door and the bar, a signed cricket bat, with the message, 'Congratulations to Chislehurst and West Kent CC, celebrating in 1988 250 YEARS OF CRICKET on THE COMMON, Chislehurst.' It was presented by Yorkshire CCC, the first-class county furthest from Chislehurst.

Between the main room and the changing rooms is the ladies' loo and a large fire-resistant safe, which obviously never contained the Ken Barrington bat. The home and visiting teams use different parts of the same changing area, which may once have been different rooms but is now one large rambling depository of hooks and lockers, beer barrels and abandoned cricket equipment. There are pads in the waste basket and a shower area with its own peculiar aroma which would be unlikely to attract a Good Housekeeping Seal of Approval. There is a great deal of make do and mend. And the vandals keep everybody busy. Alas, now there is nothing left which is not nailed to the ground. Even the sightscreens are padlocked together when not in use.

Darley Dale

·DERBYSHIRE·

THE TIMES of 20 December 1954 reported that 'Mr Alfred Smith was a lover of cricket and the club and ground of his native village near Matlock gave him all the pleasures of the game that he ever desired. He died last summer at the age of 82 and under his will, which has just been published Darley Dale Cricket Club comes into £5,000.'

Bob Winthrope, captain of Darley Dale and a schoolmaster at Matlock's comprehensive school, remembers Alfred Smith. 'When I was a small boy, I never dared sit on the benches in front of the pavilion because old Mr Smith would come round with his stick and make us go away. We were terrified of him.' His bequest, however, is still appreciated, although *The Times* report got it slightly wrong. Alfred Smith was a major local landowner, and he left the pavilion and ground to the club, as well as the interest on £5,000. The club is thus asset-rich but as cash-poor as many other cricket clubs. However, it has been successful on the field, winning the Derbyshire County League four times in the 1980s, so that although 'we did not use Alfred Smith's money wisely and are not a wealthy club', according to Bob Winthrope, they have the best facilities in the League.

The club dates from 1863, as the Darley Dale flag proudly proclaims, but the pavilion itself was built in 1907, twenty years after Alfred Smith's debut for the club. That club room is decorated in the time-honoured manner, with photographs of successful club teams, the oldest dating only from 1958, four years after the death of Alfred Smith. It shows a youthful Bob Winthrope at the extreme left, setting out on a career which is now over thirty years long. Alfred Smith played for Darley Dale for fifty years.

The home changing room at Darley Dale used to be the scorebox until a separate scorebox was built at the other end of the ground. To reach it you have to climb the narrow, steep and dark staircase at the back of the pavilion into a low-ceilinged wooden garret, which must be depressing for those who have failed to trouble the scorers and exhausting for those who have hit a century. Once there, it is easy to see why the home team have appropriated this room and left the opposition to fend for themselves in the well-equipped changing room downstairs. The view of the ground from the attic room is the best possible, although the size of the window means that the splendours of the view must be enjoyed on a strict rota. The view from the visitors' changing room is non existent, but at least it is next door to the showers, loos and kitchen, so the opposition tend to smell and eat better than Darley Dale.

Alfred Smith, according to *The Times*, 'had been brought up strictly. This showed itself in a lifelong opposition to Sunday play, and in his will he expresses a wish that there shall continue to be no Sunday play at Darley Dale.' However, on Sunday 7 September 1975, Derbyshire played Hampshire at Darley Dale, a match that Hampshire won to clinch the John Player League title for that year. Even though a crowd of over seven thousand watched the match, Derbyshire have never used Darley Dale again. The county club said the pitch turned too much, but I suspect it was Mr Smith turning in his grave.

Derby

·THE LUND PAVILION, THE RACECOURSE GROUND, DERBY·

THE FOUNDATION stone of Derbyshire County Cricket Club's present home was laid by the Mayor of Derby, Councillor Flo Tunnicliffe, on 23 January 1982. Next to the pavilion, named after one Joseph Lund whose part in the history of Derbyshire cricket is well concealed, the Old Racecourse Stand dominates the ground, being larger, older and architecturally more interesting than the new pavilion. Nobody has much that is good to say about Derbyshire's home, but everything is relative.

The facilities in the bowels of the Racecourse Stand, which was where the players used to change before Councillor Tunnicliffe cut the ribbon on the new pavilion, were reputedly so awful that visiting counties used to find it hard to press-gang a squad to play there. Even super-fit cricketers of the 1960s and 70s used to develop surprising injuries when the away game at Derby came up on the fixture list.

Cricket is played at Derby on about forty days a year. On other days, it becomes, in the words of Ken Tucker, the pavilion manager, a 'multi-functional operation'. I was there on one of the 325 days when cricket is not played, and the multi-functions going on included a photocopier and fax machine workshop in the Joseph Mason Paints Suite. The pavilion is unquestionably ugly and uncompromising, but also practical, informal and useful. It is not a club but a workplace for the players, and a useful facility for the business community. The cigarette machines on the landings seem almost the only remembrance of things past, an anachronism to my southern eyes which these days are more used to condom dispensers in public places than the shameless easy availability of twenty Silk Cut.

There is nothing self-important about the pavilion at Derby. 'Sometimes,' remarked Ken Tucker, 'I think it could do with a bit more discipline.' There are no entry restrictions, no dress regulations and no segregation by age or sex. Since Councillor Flo laid the foundation stone, eight years of piecemeal expansion with no overall plan have also removed what few traces of architectural and decorative discipline there might once have been. It is clearly a place where people enjoy their days, whether they are watching cricket or demonstrating photocopiers. But the cricketers come first.

The statutory picture of W. G. Grace is in the Joseph Mason Paints Suite. No county pavilion dare be without that. It would be like a church without a font or a boardroom without a portrait of the Founder. There must have been a wonderful business in supplying photographs of W. G. Grace to the pavilions of Britain, as very few are without at least one portrait of the Grand Old Man, sometimes greybearded and wearing a rather shabby frock coat, more often in the full flush of his hirsute prime, dressed in white and carrying a bat under his arm. The Derby photo was actually taken at Chesterfield, which has always given the impression of being the somewhat irresponsible younger brother beside Derby's stolid, head of the family image. Yet Derby clearly knows how to enjoy itself when the occasion arises. I enjoyed Derby, photocopier workshops and all.

Doo'cot Park

·PERTH, SCOTLAND·

SCOTTISH CRICKET owes a great deal to Bell's whisky. This magic potion is not only useful in warding off the cold winds that are all too often the major environmental feature of Scottish cricket grounds; it was also the source of the fortune of Arthur Kinnaird Bell, who used his money largely for the betterment of conditions for Scottish cricketers. The Grange Cricket Club's pavilion in Edinburgh, for example, was built largely with money granted by Mr Bell, but his main achievement is Doo'cot Park.

Since the death of Mr Bell, the ground and its environs have been owned and administered by the Gannochy Trust, a charitable foundation whose main thrust is in helping the sportsmen and old people of the area. It would be unfair to suggest that several of the local cricketers qualify under both categories. Two teams play regularly on the vast playing area at Doo'cot Park, Mayfield Cricket Club and Strathearn and Perth Northern Cricket Club, and they both play virtually for free. The Gannochy Trust charges a peppercorn rent for the use of the pavilion and ground all season, and even the groundsman Tom Wood is paid by the Trust. Mayfield have been playing here ever since the ground opened on 25 April 1925.

Times have changed since then. Mr Bell, who was apparently a strict martinet when it came to observing the etiquette of the game, did not allow alcohol into the pavilion, despite the fact that it was built out of the world's love of whisky. Originally there were no electric lights there, so that as dusk drew on players were forced to go home or to the pub rather than stay at Doo'cot, groping around in the dark. Playing at Doo'cot even without the promise of a drink at the end of the day must be close to a cricketer's Nirvana, but it surprises me that Mr Bell got away with such an edict in Scotland. 'The Scots are like that,' explained the factor John Nelson. 'Anything we play, we play socially. It's a means to an end. We always form clubs and are away to the pub.'

The pavilion is a curious but successful combination of brick and wood. The upper part of the pavilion features a sweeping bay window and balcony of local forest timber, in this case larch. Despite the depredations of several generations of woodpecker, the timbers are still the original 1925 vintage and there seems little chance of imminent collapse. The pavilion is divided into Mayfield parts and Strathearn parts, and the main viewing room is Mayfield territory. The Strathearn room at the back compensates for its lack of a view by collaring all the best pictures. A full set of Chevallier Tayler portraits of the cricketers of 1905 adorns the walls, including of course Dr W. G. Grace, whose portrait gives authority to Strathearn's room as the true centrepiece of Doo'cot cricket.

Next to the pavilion is a tiled courtyard complete with sundial and rose beds, a peaceful haven in the sunshine for spectators and cricketers alike. There is a plaque on the wall which reads, 'In memory of Jim Lackie, who died 1 August 1988.' 'He was a great friend of the club,' said John Nelson. 'He just came over one evening and sat on a bench and died.' All cricketers should be lucky enough to finish their days that way.

Edgbaston

·THE COUNTY GROUND, EDGBASTON, BIRMINGHAM·

THE WARWICKSHIRE County Ground at Edgbaston is, in cricketing terms, opulent. They are hoping to build a new pavilion within the next four years or so, even though the present one is carpeted throughout with navy blue Warwickshire County Cricket Club carpeting, bearing the club crest at one pace intervals, and is probably the only first-class pavilion in Europe in which some of the playing staff make their homes.

The ground is a maze of stands, annexes and outbuildings, to such an extent that it is difficult to work out where the pavilion stops and the rest of the ground starts. I think the pavilion is the bit which consists of the club offices, players' changing rooms, the matchday office, the TV and radio commentary position (but not the press box), the scorers' box, an old bell tower, the Committee Rooms, the Committee Dining Rooms, the players' dining rooms, the Chairman and President's Room, the Members' Room, the kitchens, the ITN box, the Club Suite, the main lobby and two flats, currently occupied by recent imports from other counties, Paul Booth and Gareth Smith. It may well once have been a beautiful building, but the additions have entirely destroyed its lines. The lobby displays not only an assortment of John Player League pennants, championship pennants and NatWest and Gillette Cup pennants, but also no fewer than three photographs of the late Dr W. G. Grace, who was not a Warwickshire man.

The players' changing rooms are large and chaotic, an improvement at least on small and chaotic, which is the norm in many pavilions. The home dressing room has a television set,

permanently tuned to *Neighbours* and the afternoon's racing, and players asleep on the lockers. I am beginning to believe that cricket tactics are no longer decided by the need to win the game but by the need not to miss the next episode of *Neighbours*.

If you are in the field for the after lunch episode, make sure you are batting by 5.30, so only two of your side have to miss the repeat. Any county captain who bats through both episodes is clearly being unfair to the fielding side and ought to have about eight points deducted. The baleful influence of Australia on our cricketing skills continues unabated.

From the cricket enthusiast's standpoint, the Members' Room is the highpoint of any visit to the pavilion, containing photographs and memorabilia of the club since its formation. A photograph of the county first XI in 1894 shows the pavilion as it then was, complete with a notice reading: 'Members are requested not to practise near the pavilion fencing.' These days I suspect the members do very little of anything near the pavilion fencing. They are all over in the Members' Bar, which is not part of the pavilion at all.

'There are so many nooks and crannies in this pavilion,' says David Goodyear, the Warwickshire curator, 'that you can go into one room and get lost for the next six months.' Perhaps that was just wishful thinking by a man who had taken several hours to give me the full tour of the place, but even after being left to my own devices, I was able to find my way out by close of play.

Fenner's

·CAMBRIDGE UNIVERSITY CRICKET CLUB·

'THIS PAVILION,' according to the legend on the foundation stone, 'which was built with the help of many friends of Cambridge University Cricket Club, was opened in 1972.' I do not mind admitting that my memories of the previous pavilion, which stood at the opposite (southern) end of the ground, tend to bias my views of the current Fenner's structure. I suppose it is all right in its way, but compared with its rival pavilion at the Parks, it comes as distant a second as the University boat race crew did through most of the 1980s. The view from Fenner's never matched the view from the Parks, but now that the western aspect contains one of the least inspiring pieces of urban architecture in Britain, the Kelsey Kerridge Sports Centre and Multi-Storey Car Park, it is hard to find any solace even in sitting with your back to the pavilion.

The pavilion of Fenner's is flanked by two pairs of loudspeakers on poles. Even from the far end of the ground, these loudspeakers assault the eye as much as the ear, and leave a more lasting visual impression than the tinted glass windows that run the length of the pavilion, or the white wooden benches along the front, together with the extra schoolroom chairs, which, on the day I was there, were set out in front to accommodate the members who came to watch the New Zealanders play the undergraduates (and eventually lose). Yet despite its lack of visual beauty, the Fenner's pavilion is far more practical than the one at the Parks. At Oxford the best seats in the ground are where the pavilion is the backdrop to the play, but at Fenner's there is no doubt that the best seats are in the

pavilion itself. It is a spectators' pavilion in a way that few manage to be, even if it fails to win the undying love of the players – mainly because their changing rooms give no view of the play, or indeed of anything at all. They are at the back of the pavilion on the ground floor, along a whitewashed brick corridor, tastefully decorated with tiles, radiators and pipes. But at least it all works.

The main room is practical if not elegant. A sign reads, 'Smokers: please use the ashtray and save the carpet. Thank you.' The carpet is made up of rust-coloured carpet tiles, which are aesthetically hardly worth saving. The bar at the end of the Long Room serves Boddingtons Bitter, Camerons, Websters and Carlsberg, so I would imagine the carpet to be in more danger from the drinkers than the smokers. Over the bar, all the University hockey club teams since 1962 are listed. Before 1962 they played hockey at Barton Road, so its pedigree pales beside the cricket elevens since 1898 which dominate the back wall. There is also a photograph of the 1948 Australian touring team, with the signatures of each member of that all-powerful squad on the mounting. Unfortunately, the ink has faded with the years, and only the signatures of Messrs Hamence, Johnston, Loxton and McCool have survived to be legible forty years on.

The Fenner's pavilion is not beautiful. It does not fit in easily with its surroundings. It is a functional building in a place where the cricket has been anything but functional for many generations. Fenner's is not what it was, but perhaps that does not matter. Perhaps it never was.

The Foster's Oval

·KENNINGTON, LONDON SE11·

KENNINGTON OVAL became the Foster's Oval on 24 August 1988, when the Surrey County Cricket Club members accepted a sponsorship package from the Australian brewers which assured the continuation of cricket at the Oval. One of the ways in which Surrey are spending the extra loot is in replacing and rebuilding many of the stands around the ground, which even the most avid Oval enthusiast (e.g. me) will admit needed attention.

To the inexpert eye, the pavilion is merely a poor man's Lord's, a downmarket headquarters for the cricket-loving Cockney. This image is to a certain extent encouraged, one might almost say Fostered, by the Surrey County Cricket Club, who are proud of the informality of the Oval. On the boundary fence is a notice which reads: 'Committee ruling – members dress: please note that shirts must be worn at all times.' The members obey this rule, albeit with some reluctance on a hot day, as they sit in front of the pavilion in the lime green bucket seats which have replaced the more traditional benches that are still to be found north of the river. The members do not wear ties. The newspapers discarded on the seats are *The Racing Post* and the *Daily Mirror*, rather than the *Guardian* and the *Sporting Life* which are draped over the back of the Lord's benches.

'The Refurnishing of the Long Room was made possible by a bequest from Leonard Rose Esq., 1979', says a plaque on the wall. The pavilion itself had been built 82 years earlier, in 1897, so the Long Room was in need of a wash and brush up by then. It still looks good. The pictures on the walls are of the great Surrey players – Jack Hobbs, Alec Bedser and the like, although the biggest portrait is that of William Eyton Roller striding down the (old) pavilion steps at the Oval. Roller played for Surrey from 1881 until 1890, so never used the current pavilion as a player, but as he lived to the age of 91, he probably spent many hours in the Long Room watching successive generations try to emulate his 1885 feat of scoring a double century and taking a hat-trick in the same match, which has never been equalled, anywhere in the world. The team dressing-rooms have recently moved out of the pavilion and into the second floor of the new West Stand, so no longer can Surrey players even emulate Roller's feat of striding down the pavilion steps, let alone his efforts with bat and ball.

The television room is now the Jim Laker Room, renamed on 10 July 1988 by Mr Laker's widow and full of memorabilia of that greatest of all Surrey spin bowlers. As in all cricket trophy rooms, there is no sense of the relative value of the various exhibits. The scorecard of Laker's incredible 19 for 90 at Manchester in 1956 is given marginally less prominence than a poem by Charlotte Field, which must be high on the list of technically and artistically unsound cricketing verse.

> Lock and Laker, the man-eating pair
> They have no mercy, Batsmen Beware
> Between them they harass and vanquish the 'Foe'
> And down come the wickets all in a row.

I will spare you the remaining six lines.

Gargrave

·NORTH YORKSHIRE·

GARGRAVE, A village just north of Skipton where Yorkshire starts to think about Lancashire and the Lake District, is a retirement village these days. It must be, I suppose, because Freddie Trueman lives there, and he has retired. But this Silver Fox demographic profile makes it difficult for Gargrave Cricket Club to field a Colts side any more, and some would say that we are seeing the beginning of the end of a fine Yorkshire League club. I hope not. The fact that Johnson and Johnson Patient Care Limited has built a factory almost opposite the ground is probably not because so many of their potential customers live a mere cricket ball's throw away, but rather because the soil hereabouts these days is better for growing medical companies than cricket clubs.

'There's many a bum has sat on these seats,' said my photographer, romantically summing up the generations of Yorkshire cricket lovers who have watched matches at Gargrave since the new pavilion and its benches were built in 1957. Certainly the gentle curve in the oak seats was eloquent testimony to the hundreds of solid anatomies that have relaxed in the Yorkshire sunshine over the years, though whether the phrase 'many a bum' correctly encapsulates the dry wit and canny cricketing judgement of the local population is open to doubt. We were told that Geoffrey Boycott scored a century here a couple of times, and both Yorkshire Gents and Yorkshire Second XI have played here in the past, so the bums have had plenty of reasons to stay sat on the seats. All the Craven and District League Finals are played at Gargrave because it is the best wicket in the League, and I suspect that the pavilion is one of the best in the League too.

Gargrave's ground and pavilion are owned by a trust, the Coulthurst Trust, which owns half a dozen grounds in the area, and for many years they used the facilities rent-free. In 1990 for the first time they have been charged rent, at the very reasonable rate of £750 a year, to be divided equally between the cricket and football clubs. But thirty years of cheap living does not prepare a club even for a nominal sum like this, and without a bar to raise funds, Gargrave CC are strapped for cash. The tea menu does not look like a very promising fund-raiser either. 'Full tea – 90p' it begins, making Gargrave's one of the cheapest in the country, and it is undoubtedly not one of the smallest. 'Coffee 25p, Tea 15p, Crisps 18p, Calypso 12p, Polo 12p,' it continues, but Mars Bars at 22p and Spanish at 4p are off. Whatever Spanish may be, there is no profit for the club in those prices. 'This week's sponsors, PW Plant Hire' is boldly printed on a notice-board adjoining the main road, but I doubt if the sponsors' money goes much beyond paying for the match balls. Running a club like this requires money as much as willing volunteers, but at Gargrave they have plenty of the latter and not much smell of the former.

Behind the pavilion is a large and highly technical radio mast. The pavilion is also used as the base for Gargrave amateur radio enthusiasts' club. If ever Gargrave look like sinking into oblivion, at least they can send out plenty of SOS messages before they go.

The Grange

·EDINBURGH·

THE GRANGE Cricket Club dates back to 1832, but the pavilion is Edwardian. In the bar is a wall clock with a plaque saying 'Grange Cricket Club 1909', and in the absence of any better clues, we may as well assume that the pavilion dates from that year. The clock is a typical pavilion clock. It has a large white face and has stopped at seven minutes past five. There is money to be made by any enterprising person who sets up as a visiting pavilion clock repairer, as the vast majority of British pavilion clocks tell the wrong time. Perhaps it is something to do with the romantic notion that time stops during an idyllic afternoon of cricket, but that theory does not really hold water. Perhaps it is something to do with the fact that pavilion clocks do not hold water, and as soon as it rains, they pack up.

To be fair to the Grange, there is another more ornate clock set in the gable above the door of the pavilion, and that one works. From the playing area, the pavilion is a splendid blue and white building partly hidden behind privet hedges and a large sightscreen, with an ancient scoreboard and seventeen steep steps to be negotiated by the returning batsman. That gives him plenty of time to bask in an ovation for an innings well played, but rather too much in which to endure the icy silence which inevitably follows an early dismissal. And as he passes under the clock, he is greeted by the terse message on the door reading, 'Please remove boots before entering the club.' Is there no respite for the poor batsman? Fortunately, the changing rooms are also reachable by a door underneath the pavilion, through which the less successful batsmen can slip almost undetected. This door is actually the main entrance for most of the people who use the club.

The Grange is not only a cricket club but also a hockey club and a squash club, and shares its premises with the Dyvours Lawn Tennis Club. There is clear evidence that, despite its imposing size, the pavilion is becoming too small to house the infinite variety of clubs which call the Grange home. 'Tennis Committee Meeting in Tennis Hut,' said a small notice on an oak-panelled door, presumably because there was no room in the main body of the pavilion; and the upper flights of the sweeping stone staircase have become a hastily improvised storeroom of old ledgers, photographs and files. Disused tables and chairs, boxes of the club's past and even a disconnected payphone lie gathering dust on the top landing.

The pavilion can be hired for meetings and functions. For a mere five pounds, anybody can hold a meeting in the Committee Room, although the rate for the Tennis Hut was not advertised. If you want to hold a function in the pavilion, the Long Room and Kitchen are yours for forty pounds. You get a good party for your money as well, if the almost deflated balloons hanging from the ceiling and streamers dangling listlessly from the piano are anything to go by. It is hard to judge the character of the Grange, which looks very staid from a distance, decked out in its newly glossed blue and white colours, but the façade hides a great deal of more boisterous activity. It is a heady blend of the genteel and the raucous, like a Tory MP with a guilty secret.

Hambledon

·BROADHALFPENNY DOWN, NEAR HAMBLEDON, HAMPSHIRE·

HAMBLEDON IS to cricket as Rochdale is to the Co-operative Movement, the place where its modern history began. No tour of the pavilions of Britain would be complete without a pilgrimage to Broadhalfpenny Down, where the Hambledon club organized and thus revolutionized cricket in the latter part of the eighteenth century. Of course, it is a less well recorded fact that the matches organized by the Hambledon club were rarely between Hambledon and another side: they were matches between the best players of the day, who played for one patron or another on Broadhalfpenny Down, with large sums of money wagered on the outcome. Some historians also assert that the Hambledon Club never played an eleven-a-side match in all its existence, so that its accepted role as the true founder of modern cricket is unjustified. But as any successful politician will tell you, the truth does not matter, it is what the world believes that counts. The world believes that Hambledon is the cradle of cricket.

There is still a Hambledon Cricket Club but, unlike their ancestors of two hundred years ago, they do not play on Broadhalfpenny Down. They play these days at Ridge Meadow, north of Hambledon, where they have a strictly utilitarian, low-slung wooden pavilion and are sponsored by Hartridge's Soft Drinks. Broadhalfpenny Down, about a mile away, is nowadays owned by Winchester College and leased to *HMS Mercury* at East Meon. Cricket is still played here, by a local side called the Broadhalfpenny Brigands, who keep the ground shipshape. There are no signposts from the village of Hamble-

don out to the cricket ground, which makes life difficult for cricketing pilgrims like myself, but eventually, however, all roads lead to the Bat and Ball Inn.

When cricket was in its infancy, the Bat and Ball Inn (prop. Richard Nyren) was the Hambledon pavilion. Nowadays, there is a small thatched wooden structure on the edge of the ground itself which serves as a rudimentary but rustically beautiful pavilion. A few feet away is the famous stone megalith with the inscription, 'This stone marks the site of the ground of the Hambledon Cricket Club c. 1750–1787.' The pavilion is barely half a cricket pitch in length and a popping-crease wide, but it is as clean and as spartan as any building owned by a public school and rented by the Navy should be. The litter bin behind the scoreboard is full, the boundary is marked by a properly blancoed white line along the whole perimeter of the field, and the outfield has been cut even shorter than an able seaman's hair. There are two elegant flagpoles in front of the pavilion, offset by a flourishing patch of stinging nettles at the back.

The cricketers of Hambledon formalized out of chaos the first team game to become an international pastime. If the Hambledon club had not existed, the MCC might never have been formed and the history of organized sports in Britain would have been very different. Team sports, even if they did go hand in hand with the growth of the British Empire, are one of the main positive cultural contributions Britain has made to the world over the past two hundred years. For that reason alone, Broadhalfpenny Down is worth visiting.

Hampton-in-Arden

·WARWICKSHIRE·

THE REASON for visiting Hampton-in-Arden was a prurient one. I was told that from the home changing rooms, eagle-eyed cricketers (and are not all Home Brewery Combined Counties League cricketers eagle-eyed?) can see into a particular upper bedroom of a house overlooking the ground, where at 5.30 every Saturday evening, a beautiful young lady changes to go out for the night, but routinely forgets to draw her curtains before slipping into something more comfortable. The impact of her undress on the cricket played at Hampton-in-Arden was, I was told, remarkable. If the skipper won the toss, Hampton fielded first regardless of any other considerations, so that they would be batting at 5.30, allowing at least nine of the players a chance to sit in their changing room and enjoy the show. Players batting at 5.29 would suddenly find themselves leaving a straight ball, or falling over in the middle of a suicidal second run, to be beaten easily by a throw from the outfield. It provided the only recorded instances of batsmen walking on appeals for lbw. Players asked to go out to bat before the show was over would happily risk being timed out. If Hampton lost the toss and were asked to bat first, the most likely outcome was a ghastly collapse, so that the whole match could be over by the appointed hour.

I soon discovered that the whole story was entirely untrue, mainly because you cannot see anything from the home dressing room, nor from the visitors' one for that matter. However, my disappointment was short-lived, because the pavilion deserves inclusion in any collection of cricket homes, even without the scurrilous rumours attached. The pavilion is probably the oldest building I have discovered now being used for a cricketing purpose, as it is a converted sixteenth-century barn, covered in ivy.

The opposition clubs love playing here. 'One club tours here every year from Dorchester. Our evenings always end with a beer-throwing contest in the pavilion. The place is dripping.' That's what Derek Ford, Hampton-in-Arden's Sunday vice-captain told me, so I'm not surprised the opposition like coming here, even if they lose. Derek also looks after the pitch and let slip the fact that the ground is a little uneven in parts. 'We save the near end tracks for the really fast bowlers we have to play against, so they lose their rhythm and their run-ups.' It is perhaps not surprising, therefore, that one of the most prominent posters on the notice-board in the pavilion is one that advertises: 'Physiotherapy – Sports Injuries, Neck Pain, Back Pain etc. Treatment Sessions for £10 each. Contact: Physiotherapy Department, Birmingham Accident Hospital.' Playing at Hampton is not just a matter of enjoying the cricket.

On the door is a large notice: 'Junior Cricket Starts Sunday 27 May 10.30. All Ages, All Standards Welcome. Coaching By First And Second Team Players.' Most of the players will not have bothered to go home after the Saturday night barbecue. That's what finally persuaded me that the story about the lady in the lingerie was not true: why bother to get dressed up to go somewhere else when the best Saturday night out is right there on your own doorstep?

Harrow

·FIELD HOUSE CLUB, HARROW SCHOOL, MIDDLESEX·

THERE ARE five cricket pavilions at Harrow School, and the grandest is the Field House Club. The Field House Club is not really a pavilion, it is a Victorian town house that seems to have turned into a pavilion despite itself. The building was bought for the school in 1884 by four eminent Old Harrovians, the 6th Earl of Bessborough, the Hon. R. Grimston, the Hon. Frederick Ponsonby and Mr William Nicholson. It was purchased on the condition that certain rooms were set aside to enable Old Harrovians to visit their school for the purpose of 'coaching and otherwise helping' boys on the Sixth Form Ground. Times have changed to the extent that coaching and otherwise helping is left to the coach Ramesh Sethi and the master in charge of cricket, Bill Snowden, but inside the Field House Club itself, you could be forgiven for imagining that nothing has changed in over a hundred years.

The building is used mainly as flats for the groundsman and other Harrow personnel, but the most exotic part is used as the visitors' pavilion. The home team change in the more prosaic First XI pavilion a hundred yards away, and it is there that lunch and tea are taken, and the names of the First Eleven cricketers are recorded on the walls. The Field House Club is where the portrait of E. M. 'Toddles' Dowson (Harrow 1895 to 1899) can be found, as well as those of Robin Marlar and Tony Pigott, both of Harrow and Sussex.

The Field House Club has always been conscious of its own history. The 'Harrow School Pavilion Records', beginning with Volume One from 26 May 1883, record the signatures of every opposition player who has used the Field House Club as a pavilion. Just in recent years, the names include Colin Cowdrey of I Zingari, Ian Botham as an MCC Young Cricketer in 1973, and show business cricketers such as Robert Powell, John Hurt and John Alderton. Going further back, the signatures of many world famous cricketers can be found, not to mention those who became judges, politicians or soldiers in later years. Next to the Records book there stands a rack of six pens and two inkpots, which still seem to be used for recording the signatures.

The largest wall of the main room in the Field House Club is dominated by an oleograph by Messrs Dickinson and Dickinson of *The Interval*, showing the assembled multitude at the Eton v Harrow match in July 1905. The painting was apparently found in a garage in Orpington, and donated to the school after the Second World War. As a work of art, it probably deserved its Orpington garage, but as a record of the pomp and pomposity of Edwardian England, it is of immense value.

Other trophies abound, mixed wildly in the jackdaw way that only old cricket pavilions can manage. There is a list of all Harrovian Blues, containing famous names such as F. C. Cobden, F. S. Jackson and A. M. Crawley. There is a baseball used at Harrow by the United States Air Force in June 1945, and there is the bat which was used by the Hon. Frederick Ponsonby in 1832 and 1833. It notes that his scores with this bat in 1832 were 0 and 0, and in 1833 just 0. This is my sort of trophy. I could donate bats like that to pavilions all over the world.

Hartley Wintney

·HAMPSHIRE·

CRICKET HAS been played on the green at Hartley Wintney since 1770, and the Cricketers pub on the northern edge of the green was the club pavilion in fact if not in name for most of those 220 years. Recently, however, the Hartley Wintney Cricket Club has got through pavilions as regularly as Henry VIII got through his wives, so I thought it wise to include the latest one in this book purely for the historical record, as it will probably have been destroyed by some unlikely act of God long before you, dear reader, have settled down to read this page.

From some time after the Industrial Revolution until 1954, Hartley Wintney CC, used a railway carriage as a pavilion, but then in that appallingly wet summer the first permanent Hartley Wintney pavilion was opened. It was a modest elm-wood structure, which underwent extension in the late 1970s, but survived as the headquarters of this thriving club until the night of 16 October 1985. In that night, it was consumed by fire, completely gutted by an act of juvenile arson which did not go unpunished. Within little more than six months, a new pavilion was built and opened in time for the 1986 season, but this too was a fated structure, and two years to the day after the fire, on 16 October 1987, the Great Storm (aka the Hurricane) blew several trees down on to the pavilion, which was entirely destroyed, apart from the gents' urinals which always seem to be the strongest parts of any pavilion. The good burghers of Hartley Wintney were not dismayed: they merely resolved to start again and build an even better pavilion.

The new pavilion was opened by Councillor Peter Carr, Chairman of the Leisure Committee of Hart District Council, on 7 April 1990. I like it. The dark slate roof looks like a hawk descending on its nest, and the elm-wood gabling brings back memories of this structure's predecessors. The clock outside is pure gilt, manufactured by A. W. Porter and Sons, Hartley Wintney. Inside the pavilion is another clock, manufactured a generation earlier by the then childless Arthur Porter of Hartley Wintney. The kitchen is the best equipped I have seen this side of the Roux brothers or the Welsh border, with gas cooker, microwave, dimmer switches and even a washing up machine. The food lives up to the equipment: make sure you never have to bowl the first over after lunch or tea at Hartley Wintney. It will only end in tears.

The walls of the main room are filled with items salvaged from fire and storm, including photographs of the Hartley Wintney teams of 1877, 1889 and 1908. The 1908 squad are portrayed outside a tent, which implies this was before the days of the railway carriage. There is also a large composite portrait of the First Class Cricketers of 1894, which includes the good doctor. The oddest items on the walls are just to the left of the main door – an eerie print of a Russell Drysdale painting of cricket in an Australian outback town, presented by the Australian Old Collegians on their 1968 tour, and a large children's poster beginning: 'Ann has an apple, Bill has a bat and ball.' We go on to learn that Queenie has a quilt, Tom has a train and William has a watering can. The morning playgroup held here does not clear everything away every day.

Hawarden Park

·HAWARDEN, CLWYD, NORTH WALES·

HAWARDEN PARK Cricket Club plays on a small ground in what used to be called Flintshire, between Hawarden Castle and the Pick Your Own strawberry farm. The cricket ground itself is fenced to keep out the livestock that grazes all around. The dominant sound at Hawarden is not the thud of bat on ball but the bleating of sheep among the thistles, and the mooing of cattle making their own contribution to the hole in the ozone layer above North Wales. The fence is electrified, which is not unusual, but the cricketing strategists at Hawarden have added an extra subtlety to fielding on the boundary by placing the switch for the fence inside the clubhouse. When the home side's star batsman hits a lofted shot towards the boundary, it would be the work of an instant to throw the switch of Gallagher's Mains Fence Energiser to ensure that no fielder who might look like making the catch stayed by the fence long enough to take it safely. I am sure that such a thing never happens, of course; and indeed that it would never cross the minds of any of the players to take such an action, which would be unworthy of any true village cricketer.

The pavilion has sturdy iron railings (not electrified) with red wooden posts and pots of geraniums marking the edge of the verandah outside. The whole collection looks as though it has been transplanted from the nearest railway station, very likely axed by Beeching back in the 1960s. The pavilion itself was originally a small wooden building which probably is not as old as the photograph of Hawarden Park Cricket Club of 1892, which bears the caption: 'This is the oldest group photograph of the club known to be in existence.' There are other photographs of the local teams of the past, the 1925 group featuring the Rev. the Hon. C. F. Lyttelton, of Cambridge University and, occasionally, Worcestershire, who was then 38 years old. He died only six years later, but there is no proof that he was electrocuted by a disgruntled opponent playing with the Fence Energiser. There is a television in the corner, a sign saying 'Koalas Next 10km' above the home dressing room door, and the late twentieth-century equivalent of a W. G. Grace portrait – a signed photograph of Geoff Boycott.

The rear part of the pavilion is a kitchen and a storage area. There are dustbins, chairs piled high, the telegraph board stowed in one corner, and all the bric-à-brac of pavilion life. A new extension, in summer 1990 consisting merely of some imposing brick foundations and empty crisp packets as evidence that workmen had been there within living memory, will no doubt one day conform to the unwritten law of our great summer game that cricket equipment and debris expand to fill absolutely the space allotted for them, as well as any other parts where you originally wanted to put a shower, or where the Second XI wicket-keeper wanted to store his tomato seedlings until next spring.

So don't take any notice of the plans the committee have for how it will be used. By the time somebody puts up a sign saying 'Visitors' over the door, it's too late. There are broken boundary boards, half a sightscreen and an umpire's coat with six old pennies in the pocket there already.

Honley

·NEAR HUDDERSFIELD, WEST YORKSHIRE·

THERE IS no particular reason why the Honley pavilion looks like a Chinese pagoda. Like Topsy, it just growed. Honley Cricket Club was founded in 1878, and moved to its present ground at Far End in 1881. For the first ten years or so, there was no permanent pavilion, so the players had to change in a canvas tent (Latin, *papilio* – a tent) which the club had bought from Hepworth Cricket Club for £16-10-0. In the 1890s, the present pavilion was built, a single-storey wooden building reflecting the stolid confidence of the late Victorian Yorkshire wool merchants, and the records show that by 1902 it was insured for as much as £120.

At some later stage, probably in the 1930s, the second floor was added to the pavilion, and it was then that the close resemblance to an Oriental pagoda emerged. Most cricket pavilions in England are like English churches, homes from home for the true believers who gather every Sunday, not to mention Saturdays and mid-week evenings, to celebrate their passion for cricket. In Honley they have a building that looks like a Chinese pagoda from the outside and the aftermath of a Vicarage Bring and Buy sale on the inside.

Upstairs are the changing rooms. They are painted a colour which once was turquoise but which now merely clashes with all other areas of paintwork on display. The basins are probably more interesting as antiques than as things for washing in, and anyway there is no hot water upstairs. The home changing room has more mod cons than the opposition one, in that it boasts a roller towel, and includes a chest containing various items of cricket kit and a suitcase with all the old scorebooks.

Below the stairs is a cubby-hole where they keep the kit. It is a Pandora's Box of cricketing all-sorts, a mishmash of pads, gloves and pots of paint. There are cricket bags, complete sets of Kwik Cricket donated by the Lord's Taverners, spare rolls of multicoloured lavatory paper and dozens of stumps. 'I had a friend who had a parrot,' explained committee member John Hutchinson, 'and he used to ask for the old stumps so he could cut them up for the parrot to sharpen his beak on. It had to be the old style stumps, because they were much harder.' Do the manufacturers realize that stumps these days are no good as parrot's beak sharpeners? What can Honley do with their vast stock of dilapidated stumps now?

The Honley pavilion has an even newer part than the second floor of the pagoda: a post-war East Wing which houses the tea room and the bar. The tea room includes a fine tribute to the mandarins of Honley cricket, a photograph of the 1952 committee. It shows seventeen men in severe three piece suits with their trophies, the Greenwood Trophy and the prestigious Hinchcliffe Senior Cup. It is good to see credit where credit is due. If ever the Chinese take up cricket in a big way, they will transform their pagodas into Gwangzhou and District League Club pavilions and on their walls will be hundreds of photographs showing an inscrutable Gang of Fourteen or so formally dressed committee men, guardians of the true power in the club, and no sign anywhere of a pair of flannels or a bat. But Honley did it first.

Hove

·THE COUNTY GROUND, HOVE, SUSSEX·

THERE HAS been cricket played at the County Ground at Hove since the 1870s. The present pavilion was begun then, but most of what we see today dates from the major refurbishment and extension completed in 1933. From a distance on a busy day, the pavilion resembles nothing so much as a Middle Eastern airport terminal building, its white cubical shape accentuated by windows along the complete length of the ground level, and corrugated iron everywhere. The 'Hen Room' on top would be where the air traffic controllers would sit if this was Abu Dhabi rather than Hove, and the advertising hoardings would be promoting National Panasonic or Canon rather than the more homespun benefits of Ruddles Beer, Stonegate Country Eggs and Sealink Dieppe Ferries.

At Hove, opinions about the pavilion are virtually unanimous. Nobody likes it. The County Secretary, Nigel Bett, cannot wait to tear it down and start all over again, and he is confident that 1992 will be the year when the demolition begins. That means the end of the Member's Bar, more reminiscent of a transport café than a county cricket pavilion, but bustling with life and the enjoyment of cricket. It means the destruction of the team changing rooms, including the bathroom in the home dressing room with the hot tap that has been dripping for at least three years. It means the redevelopment of the physiotherapy room, possibly the best on the county circuit, and it will mean the end of the Committee Room as we know it. But I have to admit the facilities would be far better in a new development. The present pavilion leaks, it has paint peeling

from the Committee Room walls, and the smartest part of the whole building is the old stabling area underneath, where the mowers and ground maintenance machines are kept. That part at least is spotless, even the old mangle for drying out the matting practice wickets and the notice tucked away behind a mower, reading 'Please Keep Off'.

When every trace of the present pavilion has gone and a new, architecturally stimulating and user-friendly building has replaced it, the memories of the present pavilion will remain, thanks in part to the efforts of Mr N. Shiyama. Mr Shiyama is a Japanese artist who, for some reason that nobody could understand, painted a view of the Sussex pavilion and ground in 1984. After he had completed his painting, it seemed churlish of the Sussex club not to buy it, so 'we paid him and he left it.' It now hangs in the Committee Room alongside portraits of the Duke of Norfolk, Sir Aubrey Smith and Arthur Gilligan, and opposite a fine photograph of one Jimmy Gilman, who never actually played for Sussex. He did die in Sussex, which gives him a pretty permanent connection with the county, and in 1900 he opened the batting for London Counties with W. G. Grace. A photograph of one of his batting partners is obviously the next best thing to having a portrait of the great man himself in the Committee Room. Cricket statisticians will be more interested in the fact that Mr Shiyama's landscape is the only view of a county cricket ground painted by a Japanese artist currently hanging in a cricket pavilion in Britain. Let's hope it survives when the brave new pavilion at Hove is built.

Huntly

·GRAMPIAN, SCOTLAND·

IF YOU want a quick sermon on the effects of the passage of time, head for Huntly, about half-way along the A96 between Aberdeen and Inverness. Huntly Cricket Club pavilion is painted olive green and yellow on a white background, the colours which, when added to black, are those of the Gordon tartan. The Dukes of Richmond and Gordon, whose ancestral home Huntly Castle is just over the boundary fence, may have been mighty warriors but they never had much colour sense. To get into the pavilion, you have to pass a sign which says, 'Please Note: Swear Box in operation 20p per oath', but once past that bloody thing, the most obvious feature of the place is the massive array of photographs on the wall.

The text for our sermon is taken from Psalm 90, verse 5. 'In the morning it flourisheth and groweth up; in the evening it is cut down, and withereth.' Most of the photographs on the wall feature Kevin Scott. In 1973, Kevin is standing at the edge of the back row, with flared flannels and long and untidy hair which unquestionably flourisheth and groweth up. The picture which hangs next to the 1973 set was taken in 1989, when Huntly marked their centenary at Huntly Park. The passage of sixteen years has not diminished Mr Scott's cricketing skills, for by this time he is seated in the middle of the front row, captain of his club. He has, however, lost all his hair. Those fine Bay City Roller locks are, in the words of the psalmist, cut down, and his hair withereth. The juxtaposition of the youthful, optimistic and hairy Kevin of 1973 with the mature, responsible and entirely bald Mr Scott in 1989 is a sober reminder to us all

of the inexorable march of time. By 1990 Mr Scott had become landlord of the town's main pub, and has now virtually retired from cricket, so is missing from the 1990 team portrait. How will the cricketers of Huntly mark the passage of time if they cannot use the thickness and extent of Kevin Scott's hair in the photos on the pavilion wall? I suppose they will have to use a clock or something.

There is a photograph, of course, of Major McKenzie Wood, MP, opening the pavilion in August 1920, but the club has been successful since well before then. There is a picture of the 1889 team which dismissed Elgin for 29 to win the Northern Cricket Association Cup, and another of the 1901 side that won the Aberdeenshire Cup. There are a remarkable number of trophies and cricketing oddities, including 'John Lillywhite's Prize Bat, presented to W. F. Maitland for the highest score in the Eton v Harrow Match 1862'. There no further details, such as on which side Maitland played (actually it was Harrow), or why the bat should now be in Huntly. Pride of place goes to a shield presented by Huntly Town Council to the club in June 1967 to commemorate their winning the North of Scotland League for five consecutive seasons, from 1962 to 1966, and the Knockout Cup for four seasons, from 1963 to 1966. That's quite an achievement, but as at the Foster's Oval where a shield reminds us of most of Surrey's seven consecutive championships, this trophy was presented too soon. Huntly did the League and Cup double for two more years in a row, in 1967 and 1968.

Huntly is a club which still flourisheth and groweth up.

Kirkby Lonsdale

·KIRKBY LONSDALE CRICKET CLUB AND QUEEN ELIZABETH SCHOOL·

SPARE A thought for all the wives, girlfriends and dogs of Britain's cricketers who watch their husbands, lovers and masters disappear inside an assortment of pavilions every summer weekend. What are they supposed to do while their man is engaged in athletic struggles? Should they take an avid interest in the match, so that at the close of play they can analyse exactly why their hero only scored two? Should they go home and mow the lawn because they know he never will? Should they volunteer to do teas just so they can wallow in that masculine aroma of used jock-straps and linseed oil?

The wives, girlfriends and dogs of Kirkby Lonsdale in Cumbria have the answer. Their cricket ground is in the cradle of a sweeping curve in the River Lune, no more than one hundred yards from the Devil's Bridge, one of the most perfect picnic and swimming spots in Britain. While cricketers chase the crimson rambler in the heat of a July afternoon, their dependants can eat, swim or relax by the river where the poet John Ruskin described the view as 'one of the loveliest in England and therefore in the world', even though the Kirkby Lonsdale pavilion had yet to be built.

Not that the pavilion spoils the view. It is a neat, concise green and white wooden pavilion, which exudes efficiency and energy. It is smart without ever being in danger of being beautiful. Everything is in its place. There is a notice on the door headed, 'Kirkby Lonsdale Cricket Club Car Boot Sale Sunday 5th August Duty Rota.' Everybody is given a job to do in neat half-hour slots from 7.30 a.m. until 5 p.m., when it is time for 'All hands to clear litter, notices etc.' Inside, the keys hang on the right hooks in the main room. 'Keys for Store Room', 'Keys for Score Box' and so on. For a small pavilion, it has a vast array of locks. This may be because it has a vast array of doors, including a spare one off its hinges leaning against the visitors' changing room wall.

Spare a thought for the children of Britain's cricketers, especially those who attend the Queen Elizabeth Comprehensive School in Kirkby Lonsdale. If you want to find sumptuous cricket pavilions, then visit the public schools of Britain. If you want to see cricket dying from neglect, visit the state schools. The pavilion at the Queen Elizabeth School (see page 11) has somehow survived into the 1990s, but I doubt if it will make the new century. What appears from a distance to be an elegant lime green structure worthy to stand comparison with any school pavilion in the country, turns out on closer inspection to be a rapidly crumbling shell. The paint is peeling, the panelled door has a hardboard patch on it, and the pillars of the verandah which once were wood are now metal pipes. There is a large crack in the concrete floor of the verandah, a faultline which puts the entire southern edge of the building in danger of collapse. Inside, there are a few stumps and half a scoreboard. On the wall is a large chart headed 'Girls Scoring Tables', which would make no more sense if it were the clue to 17 down in *The Times* crossword.

It is scarcely a mile from Kirkby Lonsdale Cricket Club to the Queen Elizabeth School, but it seems a lot further.

Lakenham

·COLMAN'S plc GROUND, LAKENHAM, NORWICH·

CRICKETERS TEND to run in families. You do not have to know much about cricket to know of the Graces, the Cowdreys, the Mohammads and the Hadlees. However, if you are looking for large and distinguished cricketing families, the place to start is Norfolk at Lakenham, where Colman's plc, the mustard makers, own the ground.

The pavilion at Lakenham was built in the 1930s, a fact that screams out from every red brick, every metal window frame and every straw of the impeccably thatched roof. A lesser man might have cheated and worked out the date from the large brass plaque in the Long Room, which states that 'This pavilion was erected in memory of Geoffrey R. R. Colman 1892 – 1935. Eton XI 1911, Oxford XI 1913–1914, played for Norfolk 1911–1930.' Geoffrey was of course one of the mustard family, but this being Norfolk, he was not the first member of his family to play cricket. He was at least the twelfth, because almost a century earlier, in the mid 1840s, eleven Colman brothers played as a team, and beat the might of Norwich.

In the year that Geoffrey Colman played his last match for Norfolk, three members of the Rought-Rought brotherhood played for the county, and two years later the first Edrich came into the side – Bill, then aged sixteen. The first team photo featuring the new pavilion, taken in 1936, includes two Edriches, and by 1947 the Edrich family could emulate the Colmans by putting out an eleven, including four first-class cricketers (Geoffrey, Eric, Brian and Bill), which was strong enough to beat the Norfolk county side.

Two Colmans died in the First World War: the Memorial Tablets tell us so. Norfolk County Cricket Club lost fourteen first-team players in the two wars, six in the First War and eight in the Second. Of these, thirteen were officers (including a lieutenant-colonel, three majors and six captains) and only one was a member of the other ranks. The families of Norfolk are clearly brave fighters. This is further borne out by the First Aid box in the kitchen, which is very much in the Nanny-Kiss-It-Better tradition of medical assistance. It contains the lid of an Optrex bottle, a safety pin, two packs of Vernaid triangular calico bandage and a half-finished tube of Dencorub. Do not sustain a serious injury here, unless you believe in stiff upper lips more than aspirin.

The whole pavilion is probably better cared for than the players are. The paintwork throughout is sparkling. The ceiling of the Long Room is unsurprisingly painted mustard yellow, but the outside metalwork is painted a rather peculiar mauvish purple. I asked the groundsman John Baker whether that was Colman's corporate colour. 'I suppose it is now,' he replied. 'Until six years ago it was blue, but we got a job lot of mauve paint and we are still using it up.' The benches outside are a tribute to Norfolk cricket's greatest and most active member, Michael Falcon. He was captain from 1912 until 1946, chairman from 1950 until 1969, and president from 1969 until his death two years later. During his time, he played with hordes of Colmans, Edriches, Rought-Roughts and the rest, but for some reason never got round to having a family himself.

Lancing College

·WEST SUSSEX·

THE AUSTRALIAN Test opener and journalist Jack Fingleton recalled his final innings in England in his 1958 book, *Masters of Cricket*. 'It wasn't a Test, nor a county game, but a game of odd bodies against Lancing College, high up on a lovely stretch of open ground, a beautiful chapel nearby, and a view that spread for miles across the Sussex Downs – the greenest of trees and fields with the sun caressingly warm in a blue sky. Far up planes droned like overladen bees. The pitch was true, the bowling friendly.'

With the possible exception of the comment about the friendly bowling, Lancing cricketers 35 years on would echo Jack Fingleton's sentiments. The Lancing pavilion is the same as it was then, still subdivided into many rooms. On the ground floor, there is a large groundsman's storage area, containing carefully arranged rows of spades, forks, hoes and rakes. There are cans of chain saw lubricant, keys hanging in labelled rows from cupboard doors and pristine signs saying 'Please Keep Off The Grass'. It is the neatest and cleanest room in the building. The main focus of the ground floor, however, is the Hilder Room, named after Alan Hilder, 1901–1970, who was for many years the driving force in OL sport.

Most school pavilions have a Long Room which contains photographs and/or team lists of all the First Elevens since the school, cricket or time began, whichever was the most recent. The Hilder Room at Lancing has an interesting variant on this routine. It begins its photo gallery in 1875 but misses out years which are considered by the picture editors to be of lesser interest. Thus it is that the sides of the early 1960s are left undisplayed, although the famously unsuccessful 1979 squad (Played 16, Won 0, Drew 10, Lost 6) is there, probably as a warning to all those who follow rather than as a tribute to that side's unique gifts. There is no sight of W. G. Grace, though, nor of Jack Fingleton.

The ceiling revives memories of a more serious conflict, for it is pitted with shrapnel marks dating back to the time when a bomb exploded on the Upper Field during the Second World War. There is still a slight dent along the boundary line where the bomb actually landed, but there were no schoolboy casualties. The school had been evacuated to North Wales some time before then, leaving the buildings in the hands of the War Office for the duration.

The stairs are hidden away at the back of the pavilion, but once they are climbed, we enter a different world from the bustling elegance of the floor below. Upstairs there are rooms for four more teams to change, as well as showers and other assorted plumbing facilities. Each room is full of discarded pads, bats and shirts, to an extent that I have not seen elsewhere. The tidiness of the groundsman's storeroom could be a hundred miles away: we have entered a different culture where all is disposable.

The planes from Shoreham Airport still drone overhead like overladen bees in a clear blue sky, and the thatchers are still at work on the pavilion roof. Not much changes, I am pleased to say, in cricket at Lancing College.

Lord's

·ST JOHN'S WOOD, LONDON NW8·

'FOR SHEER ignorance on the subject of cricket, commend me to the Long Room at Lord's.' These words of E. W. Dawson of Eton, Cambridge and Leicestershire (1901–1979) are frequently quoted, usually by disgruntled non-members of one of the most exclusive clubs in Britain, but it is no more true than to say that for sheer ignorance on the subject of Christianity, one should repair immediately to Canterbury Cathedral. People go to church for many reasons, not always connected with religion or the desire to be good, and as Lord's is the cathedral of cricket, there are plenty of people who go there to be seen to be there rather than for the cricket. However, I never hear ignorance on the subject of cricket in the Long Room: I never hear anything. There is a sepulchral hush in the Long Room, only interrupted by a ceremonial and rather sporadic clapping from the dozing congregation if ever a wicket falls. Even when Sir Richard Hadlee was scoring his superb 86 in his final Test innings at Lord's, nobody spoke, nobody even muttered 'Good shot, sir' into his beard. Lord's is a high church, so only the formal responses are allowed.

All the same, I love the Long Room. It is such a hotchpotch of cricketing memorabilia and imperturbable impracticality that it would be a hard man indeed who did not warm to it. The portraits of Thomas Lord, W.G. (of course), Plum Warner and Gubby Allen are there as expected, but so are those of R. D. Walker (Oxford University and Middlesex), E. Moutalt-Maude of Jersey, and my favourite, William Rice (no relation), painted by R. Scaldan in 1744. There are Staffordshire pottery figures of Julius Caesar (the cricketer, not the Roman Emperor) and George Parr, and the ball with which Ted Dexter took 5 for 8 for the Gentlemen against the Players at Lord's in July 1957.

Lord's is the headquarters of Middlesex CCC, as well as of cricket in general, which means there is a certain duplication of effort here and there. Thus there are Rolls of Honour for the MCC and Middlesex, and also for the Free Foresters and Incogniti. The late Capt. Sholto Douglas, Lt. L. J. Moon and Major R. O. Schwartz were members of the lot. There are also President's Boards, with rather fewer names recurring, and on the 'Messages to Members' board there is the clear statement that 'whilst inside the Pavilion, Members and their guests shall wear either a suit, or jacket/sports coat and acceptable trousers.' Among the types of trousers deemed to be unacceptable are 'jeans and their close relations'. Jeans and their even more heretical close relations, track suit bottoms, are the norm in most other pavilions, but the Catch-22 that MCC members face is that if they turn up unacceptably dressed they will not be able to get to the Members' Notice Board to discover why they are being excluded. I am anyway suspicious of any organization whose colours are mustard and tomato setting itself up as an arbiter of public good taste and decorum.

If the Church of England is the Tory Party at prayer, I suppose the MCC is the Tory party in whites. But Lord's is none the worse for that. For the sheer splendour of cricket, for the pomp and circumstance of sport, I commend you to the Long Room at Lord's.

Mullion and Porthcurno

·MULLION CRICKET CLUB, CABLE AND WIRELESS EXILES CRICKET CLUB·

MULLION CRICKET Club has almost certainly the most southerly cricket pavilion (see page 11) on mainland Britain, being almost at the foot of the Lizard peninsula, and the Cable and Wireless company field a few miles away could possibly contain the most westerly pavilion in Britain. I am not entirely sure of either of these facts, but these two clubs do show that even in the most extreme regions of Britain, cricket pavilions conform to a few basic rules.

The first rule is that most pavilions are not very pretty to look at. This rule applies most particularly in Cornwall, where the locals obviously feel that the rugged beauty of the landscape does not need to be enhanced by any decent architecture. The Cable and Wireless pavilion at Porthcurno is a white wooden shed with a bitumen roof, while at Mullion they began with a boxlike structure which they extended in 1985 to create a boxlike structure with an odd bit on the end.

Rule number two is that there is no normal position for a pavilion on the cricket ground. Unlike the rest of the world's great religions, cricket does not insist that all its places of worship face the same way. At Porthcurno the pavilion is facing east, and at Mullion it faces south-west. An extensive analysis of the direction which pavilions face has led inexorably to the conclusion that pavilions face all directions. There is no link with the prevailing wind (which blows lustily straight at Mullion's front door), or the evening shadows, or even with where the road and the car-park are. Pavilions are put wherever their builders can find a fairly level piece of ground or wherever

they are least visible from their landlord's window. Where the cricket is being played has nothing to do with it.

The views at Porthcurno and Mullion cannot be described as glorious on all sides. At Mullion, the view is of uninteresting houses with breeze-block garden walls and a few trees, with helicopters buzzing interminably overhead to and from the Royal Navy base at Culdrose. On one side of the Porthcurno ground the view is of the English Channel as it turns into the Atlantic Ocean, a mixture of deep blue and grey, topped by skies which on a good day are the palest blue, but too often fill with clouds the colour of Cornish slate.

One of the reasons I like the Mullion pavilion is that I am co-holder of the record for the biggest hit ever seen at the ground. By co-holder, I mean that I was the bowler off whom the blow was struck. The Mullion pavilion is as good a place as any to try to forget life's little tragedies, as the bar is usually full and friendly, and the kitchen boasts a deep fat chip fryer, which is a rarity indeed in a pavilion.

The Porthcurno pavilion has a notice which encapsulates the resignation and despair of Do-It-Yourself cricketers who have over many generations struggled to maintain and improve the quality of the working parts of a tumbledown pavilion. 'Do Not Turn Tap Off Too Tight. Drip Is Normal.' So is a bicycle in the rafters, a boat in the groundsman's store-room and a land line termination panel, bearing the proud legend 'Tablet Trunk Test 24CCT' – all of which I have seen in British cricket pavilions. That is the third rule of cricket pavilions: Everything Is Normal.

Neath

·WEST GLAMORGAN·

'A MONSTROSITY of a bar extension and ruined fascia' is how the Neath pavilion was described to me before I made the journey to South Wales to see for myself. One look at the pavilion told me the real story – the ruined fascia paid for the bar extension.

There are many grounds with advertising hoardings all around, from Lord's on Test Match days, when the going rate for a boundary board must be even higher than the cost of a gin and tonic in the Tavern, to Kirkby Lonsdale with its chalked message 'Today's Sponsors: The Apple Shop'. In Wales in particular the advertising hoarding is seen as a strong potential source of income, as at St Fagan's and St Helen's where mighty forests have been reduced to pulp in order to promote a variety of sponsors' wares to the unsuspecting spectator. I have always had my doubts about the efficacy of these hoardings: after all, who knows what a Durox Supabloc is, even after several seasons of prime site display in the Grandstand at Lord's? However, if the advertisers want to shout their message from the rooftops, or at least from the upper reaches of the walls, and pay for the privilege, why should the owners of the site try to stop them?

This philosophy has been taken to its ultimate conclusion by the Neath Cricket Club Committee. It is difficult to spread the advertising message all around the ground, because the rugby club is right next door, not to mention the public swimming baths, so what they have done is to cover the front aspect of the pavilion with advertising hoardings, bearing a wide variety of messages. It is not a pretty sight. But by ruining the fascia of the pavilion, they have raised the income to pay for the bar extension. This in turn has given them more room for advertising boards, so we can assume that they will soon be able to pay for further extensions outwards or upwards as the fancy takes them. The only limit appears to be the total number of firms in South Wales. Once they have all rented space, the building will have to stop.

'NEATH WALES FUTURE TOWN NEATH' is the most prominent sign, showing that at least a small part of the poll tax collected by the local council has been reinvested in local sporting amenities. Jewson is there too, probably on a reduced rate as the supplier of the boards themselves, and there's CMB Packaging Components and Craftsman Flooring Ltd. BJ Group plc, Monk Industrial Works Division saw no reason not to join in the fun, as have NPE Neath Precision Engineering and the rather sinisterly named Nidum Commercial Bodies Ltd. (What do they do? Are they a latter-day firm of Burkes and Hares, robbing graves for commercial purposes? Or are they a model agency, supplying pretty girls for advertisements?) And then there is Travelwise, who have taken a small space in case there is anybody who feels the need to get far away from the frankly awful sight of all those advertisements on what might otherwise be quite a pleasant building. The one company I had hoped would be advertising at Neath (but isn't) is the firm of George Edwards, who have taken space along the boundary fence at Hampshire's home ground at Southampton. They are specialists in renovating cricket pavilions.

Old Trafford

·LANCASHIRE COUNTY CRICKET CLUB, OLD TRAFFORD, MANCHESTER·

THE FIRST room I strolled into at Old Trafford was the library. There was a sale going on of old and excess stock during the lunch hour of the Lancashire v Middlesex county match, and the room was packed. The library walls are a gallery of Lancashire Test players, from the Rev. V. P. F. A. Royle (one Test at Melbourne in 1879, in which he was the first victim in the first ever Test hat-trick) to Atherton, Fairbrother and DeFreitas in 1990. It seems almost unnecessary to add that the library contains an impressive range of cricket books, yearbooks and magazines, although the range in the library was a little less impressive by the end of the lunch interval sale.

Those members who were not buying books during the break were in the main dining-room behind the Long Room, which is almost a caricature of the northern lifestyle. In a large room, people are sitting eating pie and chips in front of a television showing *Neighbours*. There are slot machines, swing bins and an overwhelming smell of vinegar. A motorcycle crash helmet and an anorak lie in an abandoned heap on a chair in the corner. I also found, much to my surprise, women in the Old Trafford pavilion. Clearly the reports in the southern press about the prohibition of the female sex here were greatly exaggerated. It must be only Lord's which is still holding out against people in skirts.

The Long Room at Old Trafford displays the usual array of portraits of mixed artistic attractiveness to cover the cracks in the plaster. The portrait of A. N. 'Monkey' Hornby, captain of Lancashire and England in the 1880s, shows the great man wearing an MCC tie, which seems a pity. Perhaps he knew that there would be red roses everywhere else in the pavilion, so nobody would mind if there weren't any on his tie. The carpets are a deep red rose pattern and the wallpaper takes up the same theme. At least the pie and chips were a standard colour.

The smartest parts of the pavilion are the Committee Room, the President's Room and the Trafford and Lancaster Suites upstairs. There's a lot of money here. The private suites in the pavilion are almost opulent (red rose carpets and curtains), although it would be unfair to suggest that the committee thinks of their own comfort first. The rest of the pavilion is also being given a full face-lift, as can be deduced from the notices every five yards apologizing for 'lack of facilities during refurbishing'. I found the facilities eventually, downstairs just as they are at Lord's and the Oval. The facilities for the other (supposedly banned) sex are officially designated 'Ladies Powder Room', but they are hidden away along a side corridor past a row of payphones.

The Old Trafford pavilion is only for members and players. The museum is tremendous, but in another part of the ground. The club offices are for the time being in a Portakabin or two in the car-park, as part of the face-lift process, and the Pennines are still where they always were, somewhere behind a raincloud to the north of the ground. The pavilion has no diversions (apart from pie and chips). It is there for watching the cricket, because the pitch is the only direction you can turn unless you sincerely wish to be overwhelmed by red roses.

The Parks

·OXFORD UNIVERSITY CRICKET CLUB·

IF LIFE is treating you harshly, or if you feel you deserve a day of pure self-indulgence, a warm early summer day at The Parks is the answer. The setting is perfect: a wide open space in the heart of the city of Oxford, a city which never quite bustles although it would like to give the impression that it does. Around the ground is a rope which separates the paying public from the passers-by, but as far as I could tell the only paying to be done was forty pence for a scorecard.

The pavilion and its setting are indivisible. It is a leisurely, civilized place. The birds sing politely in the trees behind the scorebox and the flags hang limp in the sunshine. The pavilion itself is the archetypal Golden Age pavilion, built in 1881, and virtually unchanged since. Only a television aerial on the chimney-stack betrays the influences of the twentieth century. It is, however, one of the few pavilions which are more appreciated from outside than in. From inside the pavilion and the members' enclosure, you cannot enjoy the ornate simplicity of its architecture, the white wood pillars proving that an artistic eye can do something even with blocks of wood, and the three gables with the clock set firmly in the centre gable. Inside the pavilion, the afternoon sun shines into your eyes, making it a strain to watch the cricket.

On the southern edge of the pavilion, the OUCC offices show the influence of the Portakabin school of architectural design, and behind them the city of Oxford in the distance throws up a cocktail of fourteenth-century colleges and twentieth-century multi-storey car-parks. The pavilion is more in harmony with its surroundings than any of these other buildings which catch the eye across The Parks. Inside, however, the pavilion is a disappointment. There is one main room, where meals are taken, a press box and a kitchen on the ground floor. The undergraduates change in the basement, from which the pitch is entirely invisible, and the visitors in a little shack between pavilion and scorebox, aptly called 'The Hut'.

The main room of the pavilion has painted on its walls the names of every Blue XI since the first match against Cambridge in 1829, a habit that has spread to many other pavilions, and a small plaque over the fireplace, which reads: 'This room was refurnished in 1950 in memory of Frederick Crawford Boult, Lieutenant Grenadier Guards, captain of Oxford University Cricket Club XI in 1941, who was killed in action in Tunisia on May 3rd 1943.' The refurnishing seems a little sparse forty years on. What we have now are rows of tables with functional chairs to match, supremely ugly views out of the back windows on to lawn-mowers and rolled-up matting wickets stored in large sheds, and the sound of Radio One blaring from the kitchen. The groundsman's offices are hidden away up stairs studded by generations of cricket boots. The best views from the pavilion are reserved for the ground staff.

The pavilion at The Parks is one of the most beautiful in Britain, but it is a celebration in architecture of the spirit of cricket, not a working building. The best advice is to lie in the sunshine by the trees on the southern edge of the ground and admire the pavilion from afar.

Reepham

·LINCOLNSHIRE·

'I LOVE VILLAGE CRICKET, FOX AND HOUNDS REEPHAM' is the bold declaration on the sticker on the front door of Reepham's small pavilion. A sign on the side of the pavilion, where it edges very close to the house beyond the boundary, has a more austere message: 'DON'T PLAY CRICKET NEAR THIS FENCE'. Obviously not everybody shares the opinions of the management of the Fox and Hounds.

The land around Reepham Cricket Club's ground is farmed by the president of the club, Philip Good. The ground is used not only for cricket, but also for the local primary school sports, as evidenced by the 100-metre running lanes marked out in the grass, which was still very green in late May. Some of these primary school athletes are regular visitors to the ground at an even earlier stage in their lives, it appears. The story is told of the wife of a Reepham cricketer in primmer days before the Sixties made bodily frankness obligatory, who was loyally watching her husband making a few runs when she realized it was time to feed her newborn baby. Where better to find a little privacy for the intimate innocence of breast-feeding than the visitors' dressing room while they were fielding? She and her infant had settled down to the task amid a masculine still life of discarded shirts, socks and worse, when a sudden downpour sent the teams running for shelter. Mother was covered in embarrassment but little else, but the child was not to be diverted from its feed. Expanding the population and eating have always been essential parts of the lives of village cricketers, so the visitors just moved in to the home dressing room and let this demonstration of one of the great mysteries of pavilion life continue undisturbed.

There is no electricity in the pavilion, although there is Calor gas and running water in the main room, which acts as tea-room, kitchen and waiting room for the players and their loyal supporters. The Tea Ladies Calendar is hanging on a nail in the wall. The home changing room is not the most elegant in England, but it contains all the essentials for those needing to change from their everyday Clark Kent outfits into their cricketing Superman white shirts, flannels and boots (except a phone booth, I suppose). There are hooks on the wall, benches to sit on and team photos to gaze at. There is also a cutting from *The Sunday Times*, dated 1982, of an article by Robin Marlar on the intricacies of the lbw law. It seems that there is as much uncertainty and deep feeling in Lincolnshire about this recondite aspect of cricket as in other pavilions around the British Isles, where similar notices are prominently displayed.

Reepham pavilion is white with green trimmings, and very well cared for. The name of the match ball sponsor is displayed on a board at every game, but most of the names seem to be unnecessarily industrial for so idyllic a ground. We can only assume that the connection between industry and village cricket is mutually beneficial: the cricketers get their ball paid for, and the industrialists have the chance to spend a peaceful summer afternoon under the trees at Reepham, watching village cricket. Let us hope that some of the industrialists take up this opportunity that their small generosity has afforded them.

St Fagan's and Freuchie

·ST FAGAN'S CRICKET CLUB, NEAR CARDIFF, SOUTH GLAMORGAN AND
FREUCHIE CRICKET CLUB, FIFE, SCOTLAND·

ST FAGAN'S won the National Village Championship in successive years, 1981 and 1982. They boast a very large ground, their trophy cabinet is as well stocked as their bar, and the piano looks as though it has survived several noisy Saturday nights. The only problem is the pavilion itself, which is of the Snowcemmed Portakabin school of cricketing architecture, and not beautiful. There is a small sign on one wall with the plaintive message, 'Keep Off Roof'. Most people need little encouragement to obey.

It was not always thus, and to give them their credit, it will not stay thus much longer if St Fagan's have their way. Plans for a new building are pinned to a notice-board in a place which is known as Bullshit Corner. A sign proclaims the area where the players can explain away their failures of the weekend over a pint or two, but I am sure that the plans for a new pavilion are more firmly based on reality than the claims and counterclaims of disgruntled cricketers. 'It's difficult to get near the bar some evenings,' said one player. 'They take over the whole corner.' St Fagan's are lucky they can limit the bullshitters to just one corner. In most clubs they cover all available floor space, often horizontally.

I had not intended to visit another National Village Championship winner, but on the recommendation of David Gower ('I had a good evening there a few years ago'), I changed my itinerary to fit in Freuchie. I am glad I did. The first photograph on the wall of the pavilion which caught my eye was of a relaxed David Gower, beer glass rather than champagne flute in hand, perched on the edge of a bar stool, as proof not only of the good evening a few years ago but also that great cricketers have a fine sense of balance.

Freuchie are a very successful village side. They have been Village Championship Scottish Champions in 1976, Group Champions in 1986, 1987 and 1989, Group Runners-Up in 1988, and National Quarter-Finalists in 1982 and 1990, yet their trophy cabinet only emphasizes their *annus mirabilis* of 1985. That year, as well as being National Village Champions, they were voted Scottish Television Team of the Year (a big silver salver), BBC Scotland Sportscene Team of the Year (a cut glass bowl) and winners of the Wilkinson Sword Trophy (a sword large enough to make Excalibur look like a fish-knife) for the Best Sporting Achievement of the Year.

The scorebox is used as a repository for worn-out equipment: an old cricket bag, two bats and a broken MaxiCool wine cooler, which explains why David Gower was drinking beer that night. On the other hand, the Simms-Watts P.A. 2000 Super Machine and two speakers looked in fine working order. Their banishment to the scorebox is more likely explained by the hand-written notice on the wall of the Lounge: 'Bands – Discos: Due to a complaint to the *Police* by neighbours of the club, we ask you to keep your music to a level to be enjoyed by the members inside, and not be heard outside. Thank you.' As the members at St Fagan's would agree, a good club is a noisy club.

St Helen's

·SWANSEA, WEST GLAMORGAN·

THE PAVILION at St Helen's is a pavilion of two halves, Brian, the two halves being rugby and cricket. And if you know what I mean, Brian, at the end of the day the rugby half is bigger than the cricket half. The club is called the Swansea Cricket and Football Club (complete with coat of arms and complicated Latin motto, Floreat Swansea), but that order of words is just to lull cricket members into a false sense of security. This is a rugby ground where they also play cricket. It may be the cricketers, not the rugby players, who are daunted by the infamous 67 steps up from the playing surface to the dressing-rooms at Swansea (which used to be 89 steps until the recent redevelopment, and which seem like 289 when you have been out for very few), but nevertheless this is rugby country.

From the outside, it could be anything. The external walls of the pavilion are covered with such stimulating messages as 'DP Fit For Life' and 'City of Swansea Central Works Unit City Engineer's Department WORKING FOR YOU.' There is nothing which tells you that you are staring at the outside walls of a sports pavilion. The main entrance has a tablet which 'commemorates the achievement of George Ll. Hay Esq., Life Vice-President of the Swansea Cricket and Football Club, who by his untiring efforts collected the funds for the erection of this pavilion 1930.' The main staircase from the hallway to the first floor is obviously undergoing some renovation. The first-floor landing has become half trophy room and half warehouse. There is a piano (all Welsh pavilions except Abergavenny have a piano somewhere, although most are in slightly more

accessible places than a first floor landing), an unplugged space invaders game and a board listing the names of 'Captain's Choice' award winners in football, hockey and cricket. The board confirms Welsh sentimentality by quoting Grantland Rice's immortal couplet from his poem 'Alumnus Football' about the one Great Scorer marking not what you won or lost but how you played the game. I knew I would find that in some British pavilion if I looked hard enough.

The Members' Bar, to which I needed to repair for a stiff drink as an antidote to the overdose of Great Scorers, is a rugby club bar. There are rugby club shields all around, and rugby photographs. There is no portrait of W. G. Grace or Don Bradman anywhere to be seen. I climbed the stairs once again in search of proof that cricket exists in South Wales.

The top floor of the St Helen's pavilion restored my faith in Welsh humanity. I will even overlook the fact that the president of the Welsh Rugby Union opened the Roof Bar and the executive entertainment suites, because they were opened in mid-April 1990, just in time for the cricket season but too late for rugby. They are truly magnificent, fitted out in sumptuous style and with views on a clear day right across the Bristol Channel to the Devon coast. I even found some framed cigarette cards of cricketers on the wall of one of the executive suites. If you want a panoramic view of cricket (or rugby, I must reluctantly admit), then I cannot believe there is a better one anywhere in the country than from the top floor of the St Helen's pavilion. Floreat Swansea, indeed.

Saltwood

·SALTWOOD CRICKET CLUB, HYTHE, KENT·

THE WHITEWASHED wooden pavilion at Saltwood, a village on the fringe of the Channel Tunnel excavations in south-east Kent, cannot rival Lord's for architectural magnificence, but it has its own individual appeal, especially among masochists. The setting is splendid. The sinister Norman Saltwood Castle can be glimpsed through the trees on the northern edge of the ground, and the bright blue of the English Channel spreads out to the south. On a clear day with binoculars and standing on the highest branches of one of the few trees to survive the Great Storm of 1987, you can even see the coast of France.

The pavilion has no name. Perhaps there has been no benefactor of the club who ought to have been remembered by having the pavilion named after him, but more likely there have been several such benefactors who have all turned down the honour. Would you wish to be immortalized in wood and plasterboard, with primitive semi-external plumbing?

Until 1990, the kitchen contained the most dangerous item seen at a cricket match since Bodyline, namely a hot water boiler. This was officially safe in the way that a circus lion is safe, but it needed a fully qualified trainer with whip and chair to get it to work properly. The tea ladies of Shepway were celebrating for days when the new stainless steel urn was installed in the spring of 1990. Saltwood benefits from having a plumber on its committee, which means that major technological developments such as this and a new shower make their way into the pavilion almost as soon as they are announced, or at least within ten years of their first appearance at the Ideal Home Exhibition. The shower arrived in 1988, displacing the ladies' loo, which was united with the gents' in a display of sexual equality not necessarily appreciated by everybody. Nobody uses the shower except opposition players who have not tried it before, but as the shower adjoins the home changing room, the home side have to put up with a stream of naked opponents invading their privacy, sweaty and optimistic on the way in, soaking and disillusioned on their way out after fighting a losing battle with one of the most recalcitrant showers in Britain. It is likely to be the only defeat the opposition will have suffered that day.

As they shuffle back to the visitors' changing room, taking care to avoid splinters from the original wooden floor, they pass the beautifully painted message on the wall, 'Give of Your Best for the sake of Giving, & not for what You can get out of the Game for Yourself – Major Oliver Villiers M.C.' Back in their changing-room, the message on the wall is a rather less inspirational one – 'Visitors' Teas £11'. Generations of Saltwood players have heeded Major Villiers' advice, having given their best, but getting little out of the game for themselves. They did win the Kent Village League 3rd Division in 1987, but apart from that the trophy cupboard is rather bare. It would be a typical friendly village pavilion if it was not for the framed scorecard on the far wall which tells of the match between Saltwood and Martin Walters' XI on 23 May 1964. Saltwood scored 216, and then dismissed Mr Walters' entire side for 0. Not many clubs can boast success like that.

Scarborough

·NORTH YORKSHIRE·

THERE IS only one real cricket festival left in England, and that is the Scarborough Festival. Other places, such as Canterbury and Cheltenham, have their festival weeks, but Scarborough is the only place where they still play true festival cricket. The Scarborough ground is slap in the middle of the town, almost completely hidden by the surrounding rows of terraced houses, so that finding the place is a festive occasion in itself. Once inside the ground, the tang of sea air dominates (or maybe it was just the prawn cocktails we had for lunch), but despite the smell, the tents and the flags, this is a more urban ground than any other I have been to – more so than Trent Bridge, the Grange in Edinburgh, or even Bath.

The cricket ground was there before most of the houses. The club was founded in 1849 and the present pavilion was built in 1895. It cost about £2,000, much less than the Lord's pavilion which cost £21,000 five years earlier. I know that because Scarborough Cricket Club has made sure its every move these past 140-odd years has been well documented. Their archives include, for example, photographs of every president of the club since 1865. Scarborough's pavilion is an amazing repository of historical cricket photographs, and this is its charm. It has other attractions, of course, like good beer on tap, a mezzanine floor for corporate entertainment, and a one-armed bandit that actually pays out once in a while. It even boasts a hand-wound clock made by I'Anson of Scarborough, which really works, presented many years ago by the local Member of Parliament. But the photographs are what makes it all so different.

Of course, there is the compulsory picture of W. G. Grace taking pride of place on the stairs, and a fine portrait of Sir Leonard Hutton, but they are surrounded by a bizarre collection of lesser names. Why should the walls be covered in photographs of cricketers like M. M. Walford (Somerset 1946-53), E. B. Lewis (Warwickshire 1949-58) and C. T. M. Pugh (Gloucestershire 1959-62)? M. C. Cowdrey I can understand, even a very youthful A. R. Lewis maybe, but D. Kirby (Leicestershire 1959-64)? I had to ask. Scarborough's John Found told me, 'They date back to the days when there was always a Gentlemen v Players game at the Scarborough Festival. The amateurs all used to stay at the Grand Hotel, who collected photographs of the players. When Butlins bought the Grand Hotel, they found all the photographs and offered them to us as a job lot.' It seems amazing that the Scarborough committee, with such an assortment of photographs to choose from, should decorate the stair wells with a job lot of 1950s amateurs, but it is good to see them being put to some use after all these years.

The pavilion is on the northern side of the ground, so it catches the sun throughout most of the day. By early evening, the main bar is beginning to feel quite warm, and the members out on the balcony are glowing a gentle pink as the sun sinks gradually lower. The upper windows of the houses all around are filled with people getting a free look at the festival cricket, but somehow the town seems to have receded. Scarborough Cricket Ground seems to cocoon itself in its own world when the sun shines and the cricket sparkles.

Sedgwick

·SEDGWICK HOUSE GROUNDS, CUMBRIA·

THE HISTORY of Sedgwick Cricket Club, a two-page section in the 1990 Membership Card and Fixture List, concludes with the following words: 'Today the constitution reflects the importance of the Sedgwick players. Flushing toilets are to be installed this year.' The players must be pretty important to merit flushing toilets, but if the truth be known, Sedgwick were installing these marvellous devices in 1990 because they very much hoped they would be promoted to the First Division of the South Lakeland League, and First Division teams ought to have flushing toilets in their pavilions.

Even without the sophisticated plumbing, Sedgwick Cricket Club's pavilion is a lovely place. It is set in the grounds of Sedgwick House, which until the Second World War was owned by one Jacob Wakefield, an enthusiastic patron of country house cricket. It was the Wakefield family who originally built the pavilion. After the war, Sedgwick House became a residential home, run by the local council, and Sedgwick Cricket Club had to re-establish itself as an independent body. They swept out the pavilion, put in new panes of glass and flourished on a wicket described as one of the best in South Lakeland.

The club now has seventy members and flushing toilets going in the back of the pavilion. Progress is a wonderful thing, but it does mean that while the work is incomplete, there are unexpected hazards like open bags of cement on the floor and large plywood and gyproc rectangles stacked against the wall in what would otherwise be a very attractive main room. The olive

green and gold paintwork (Club Rule 19: Club colours are green and gold) looks more like olive green and black at the moment. It will need a bit of touching up once the toilets are in full flushing order. The List of Century Makers board on the near wall is a little dusty and partly obscured, although we can still read the names of G. E. Webster, who in 1893 scored the first ever century at Sedgwick House, 106 against Old Sedberghians, and E. Garnett of the Free Foresters, who scored 171 against Sedgwick in 1898 – still the record score here. The most recent addition to the list is Graeme Fowler, of Lancashire and England, who scored 115 for Paul Allott's XI in a benefit game early in 1990.

There is still no electricity in the Sedgwick pavilion. It would be very expensive to wire the place up, and they do have a gas cooker at least. The Horse Manure Competition on 26 May advertised in the fixture list could be an attempt to find an alternative method of power generation, or it may just be Sedgwick's answer to St Fagans' Bullshit Corner.

Sedgwick Cricket Club's Constitution and Club Rules, dated February 1990, begin:

'1. That the club shall be called Sedgwick Cricket Club.

2. The object of the club is the playing of cricket.'

There are 24 more rules after that, but you don't need to read them. Here at last is a club who only want to play cricket, and who are lucky enough to do so in the most elegant surroundings. Flushing toilets and First Division cricket will not, I sincerely hope, change that.

Titwood

·CLYDESDALE CRICKET CLUB, TITWOOD, GLASGOW·

SCOTLAND'S NATIONAL cricket centre is the Clydesdale Cricket Club at Titwood, on the southern edge of Glasgow, or at least that is what the club tells me. The members of the West of Scotland club at Hamilton Crescent just the other side of the Clyde might disagree, but I've been to them both and I reckon the Titwood people are right. If Scotland has a Lord's (and thank goodness it hasn't, many would say), then Titwood is the place and Clydesdale Cricket Club is its MCC.

The club was founded in 1848 by Archie Campbell from Hawick, who sounds Scottish enough to me. They moved from their original ground at Kinning Park in 1871, when they sold the place to a struggling football club called Rangers. The link with football and Rangers remains, and Clydesdale are proud of their record of being the only cricket club to have played in the Scottish Cup Final. They lost 2–0 to Queen's Park in 1874. The pavilion, an imposing white building with seven rows of brown wooden benches outside, was built in 1904, before the undistinguished terraced houses which now overlook it were even a twinkle in the town planner's eye.

Until 1974, the only place you could get a drink in Scotland on a Sunday and on other occasions when the pubs were shut was in a licensed club such as the Clydesdale Cricket Club. In those days, there were a lot of drinking members, who occupied the chairs facing the bar rather than the benches outside, but now that licence has been applied to Scotland's licensing laws, membership at Titwood is down to around three hundred. It is among the keenest, most dedicated and most lively mem-berships of any club I have gatecrashed, strip clubs and Neighbourhood Watch Associations included. On a mid-week late afternoon, the pavilion was bustling, the bar was open and the pool table in operation. Outside, the preparations for an evening match were almost complete, to such an extent that the only way I could conduct the interview I needed with Mike Stanger, the Titwood ground convener, was to walk round the perimeter with him, adjusting the boundary rope and pushing the sightscreens into place. The long Scottish evenings mean that much of the cricket played here begins at six o'clock on mid-week evenings, and even fast bowlers are visible until almost nine o'clock. Apart from the super-fit athletes and old lags who form the three adult elevens, some seventy boys between eight and eighteen play regularly in junior sides at Titwood, which is a superb way to begin a cricket career.

I was assured that in the pavilion you could chance upon the wittiest, most erudite cricketing observations you could ever hope to hear, but the two examples I was given obviously required so much intelligence or so much whisky to be comprehensible, that I will not risk repeating them here, as I am sure I could not do them justice. Or perhaps it is the accent.

There is no photograph of W. G. Grace, but there is a trophy cabinet and a bar, both well-stocked, and over a door there is a cricket stump with the head of a golf club screwed into it, bearing the legend: 'The CCC Stump, presented by N. W. Turner.' Titwood would not be a Scottish cricket club if it did not have a golfing trophy in there somewhere.

Trent Bridge

·NOTTINGHAMSHIRE COUNTY CRICKET CLUB
TRENT BRIDGE, NOTTINGHAM·

THE PAVILION at Trent Bridge, the home of Nottingham-shire County Cricket Club, is the third on that site. It was completed in 1886, and thus is the oldest of the major first-class pavilions in England, and four years older than that yardstick at Lord's. Extra bits were added in 1953, and an Executive Box was built on to accommodate the corporate sponsorship boom of the 1980s, but the pavilion remains essentially an ancient building, almost prehistoric in cricketing terms.

Trent Bridge is a curious blend of 1980s commercial acuity and 1880s cricketana. The Executive Suite on the top floor of the pavilion is for people who know nothing about the game but who appreciate the chance to drink all day on somebody else's budget. Executive members gain access to a large room with green baize chairs, a murky green carpet and a peculiar if not entirely objectionable smell. The view is of high-rise office blocks in the centre of the thriving city of Nottingham, and of Nottingham Forest and Notts County football grounds. County members have to concentrate on the pleasures of the rest of the pavilion, and the view of the cricket. The boundary fence in front of the pavilion announces that 'This fence was donated by Nixon Knowles & Co. Ltd., Timber and Plywood Importers, Queens Drive Industrial Estate, Nottingham.' If any of the Nottingham members need several hundred yards of white picket fencing, they know where they can buy it.

When rain stops play, there is a choice between the bar and the museum. The former, which doubles as a Long Room, has many fine old bats in serried ranks above the bar, and a large £3,000 television. But it is the museum which is the real joy for the cricket lovers of Nottingham. It was originally the groundsman's bedroom, and the present pavilion manager Harry Dalling used to sleep here as a child, when his father was ground superintendent. It has been a museum since Saturday 9 May 1987. Among its photographs of Famous Nottinghamshire Batsmen is one E. E. Hemmings, whose photograph was in the Famous Bowlers section until the day after Mr Hemmings squirted John Lever for four off the last ball of the 1989 NatWest Trophy Final to bring the title north.

The Committee Room is best avoided by lovers of simple good taste. Yellow plastic roses adorn the committee table, and a wood carving of the ground's founder William Clarke in a top hat tries to merge with the scenery above the bar. The room is used extensively: there is a full committee meeting once a month and 'a tremendous amount of sub-committees' – none of whom, unfortunately, have yet voted to chuck the yellow plastic roses into the rubbish bin.

The players' dressing rooms are far more in keeping with the spirit of William Clarke. They are clean, simple and in two parts, with doors taken out to give the impression of a unified whole, but in reality they are a merged version of the pre-1963 separate amateur and professional changing rooms. The whole of Trent Bridge is a merger of the new and the old orders, but it is a merger that works.

Truro and Falmouth

·TRURO CRICKET CLUB AND FALMOUTH CRICKET CLUB·

CORNISH CRICKET pavilions are memorials to the past. Perhaps there is something in the Cornish character that prefers to dwell on the glories and romance of days gone by, or perhaps the man who built Truro Cricket Club's pavilion (see page 11) at Boscawen Park was a monumental mason in his spare time. In front of the pavilion is a slate wall with what looks suspiciously like a marble tombstone on top of it, bearing the inscription: 'The Ray Roberts Enclosure'. The enclosure itself is a small lawn bordered by a well stocked and well tended flower bed, just like a Garden of Remembrance. All over the walls of the pavilion are further reminders of Truro's past. 'This stone was laid on behalf of past and present members of Truro Cricket Club by Francis J. Radmore – life member and Richard L. Frank – president, 28th July 1960'. 'The weather vane was erected in 1988 in memory of J. R. Slater and G. N. Slater, life members who served this club for many years'. 'These facilities were provided with the help of a grant from the National Playing Fields Association'. Even the clock (which seems to be working) is 'in memory of R. L. Frank Esq. President 1959-64'. The wooden benches, too, are dedicated to past members, and the only sign I could find that did not point out the mortality of man was the one in the window of the new extension, which read 'Bar Open'. It wasn't.

At Falmouth the entire ground is a memorial. It was presented to the club in memory of William Edgar Hawkey, and opened by Mr Hawkey's widow on 25 April 1953. The ground was carved out of a hillside to create an amphitheatre, with the pavilion dominating the high ground. Falmouth's pavilion is only seven years older than Truro's, but, despite frequent improvements and extensions since 1953, it looks a generation older. Falmouth believes in the standard, single-storeyed, long white box style of pavilion construction, with room to get longer but no less box-like as the years go by. Truro has built a two-storeyed structure with massive window panes, spindly pillars of metal rather than wood, and an angular design which is as Sixties as Twiggy or a civil rights march. Falmouth, which dates from that forgotten age before Her Majesty's Coronation Day, has nothing but benches outside (several in memory of Ralph and Noel Dorning), where Truro has rows of blue 'Restall' stadium seats. What's more, they are well spaced so that taller members can sit comfortably in them.

Both clubs have recently added an extension which has improved their bar facilities, at Falmouth with the help of a loan from the Redruth Brewery four years ago. Newquay Steam Bitter is the beer on tap, but there is also a trophy above the bar (next to the Eric Haselum Memorial Clock) for the 'Courage Best Sports Quiz League Champions', so at Falmouth they must be free with their alcoholic favours. At Truro, the bar has been completed much more recently, and in the autumn of 1990 they were still waiting for planning permission approval 'to construct a septic tank to serve new bar, store and toilet'. It is to be hoped that planning permission is speedily granted because, if not, another hot summer could create major atmospheric problems downwind of Boscawen Park.

Westminster School

·VINCENT SQUARE, LONDON SW1·

WHEN I arrived at Vincent Square, during the Westminster School v MCC match, the groundsman Ray Gilson was repairing a door handle on the new home shower room, which had proved inadequate for the effort demanded of it. 'Look at those screws,' he said, pointing at a couple of stubs which were supposed to secure a heavy gold-plated doorknob to a door which is opened and shut scores of times during any match day. 'No good to anybody.'

The same would certainly not be said of the Vincent Square facilities as a whole. The ground is an oasis of greenery in Pimlico, a patch of ground owned by the Church Commissioners and made over to the school for recreational purposes only. The ground is not only used by the schoolboys: the Old Boys play there in the summer, the Cricketer Cup final is played there, and there were to be a couple of games later in the summer as part of Paul Downton's benefit year. Not only Westminster, but also the Abbey and Cathedral choir schools use the ground, while the Lords and Commons XI, who play as the visitors against both the school and the Old Boys, are allowed in alternate years to act as hosts to the Dutch Parliament XI. It is a lively, friendly, busy place.

The pavilion was built in 1871, according to the archaeological evidence of a cast iron hopper on a downpipe, and was restored in 1949 'as part of the War Memorial of Westminster School'. In the dining room, built as an adjunct to the main changing room edifice, the only trophies are a poster advertising a match played by Westminster School Football Club in Italy on 25 Marzo 1987 and a Liverpool FC banner. Apparently Liverpool have often trained there when they have evening mid-week games in London. The pavilion is, of course, a home for football as well, although football is only played there six days a week in the winter. Cricket goes on seven days a week in the summer.

The school colour at Westminster is pink. Players who have earned their school colours are 'Pinks', and upstairs is an attic room called the Pinks' Room. Another of those ubiquitous pavilion plaques announces that 'The Renovation of this Room was completed with the help of a generous gift from Francis Pagan, May 1965', although whether Mr Pagan was entirely satisfied with the result of his generosity is not recorded. The walls are pink emulsion and the room is entirely bare apart from a few chairs and a fireplace with an empty cigarette packet in it. In the cupboard there are a couple of 20p Lucozade bottles full of cigarette ends. 'The lads come up to the Pinks' Room for a smoke.' I think I could have worked that one out for myself. At least the empty bottles are Lucozade rather than gin. The view of the ground from the Pinks' Room window is superb, but a better view is obtained from the other side of the ground, because from there you can see the pavilion itself and the Houses of Parliament just to the right in the semi-distance.

The roses outside the pavilion, along the pickets that separate the pavilion from the playing area, were planted by Ray Gilson and add to the rural aspect of this city centre site. They are a beautiful pink, of course.

Worcester

·NEW ROAD, WORCESTER·

A PIECE of paper pinned to the notice board at the back of the Worcester Long Room reads: 'Members and guests are required to be dressed in a generally acceptable manner when using this pavilion.' Another notice by the plate glass door leading out towards the pitch attempts to define what is acceptable in Worcestershire, by using the phrase 'smart casual'. However, 'Bare torsos do not qualify.'

Worcestershire's pavilion was built in 1898. It is beautiful and full of useful notices. There are flowers everywhere (Floral Displays by Webb's Garden Centres), and the best signposted toilets on the county circuit. Wherever you are around the ground, there will be a signpost within ten yards pointing shamelessly to 'TOILETS'. The fact that all the signs point in different directions does not matter: there are toilets a-plenty at Worcester and the authorities are determined that as many visitors as possible will use them. I have to add that once you get there they are not as elegant as some other parts of the ground, but they serve their purpose.

The Committee Room has its own bar, of course, and its own viewing balcony, with three benches dedicated to the memory of Geoffrey J. Dorrell T.D., J.P., Worcestershire County Cricket Club Chairman 1956, 1957, 1959, 1960, 1961, 1970, 1971, 1972, President 1973. There's barely room to sit down after that lot has been screwed on to the woodwork. The signwriters at Worcester are obviously paid by the word.

There is a door in the Long Room wall about eight feet off the ground above the plate glass doors. There is no indication of why the door is there, how people who are not professional basketball players reach it or what is behind it, other than a sign next to it which reads: 'These Chairs, Given By The Metal Box Company, Are Intended For The Use Of Senior Members Of The Club.' Provided they are smartly casual and not baring their torsos, of course. Across the room, by the passage towards yet another toilet, is a brass plaque some three feet above the green and pink patterned carpet, which proudly records 'Flood Level March 1947'.

At New Road a rowing boat is kept handy for the use of the groundsman in the early months of the year. I assume the pavilion carpet is waterproof.

There are several more normal items on display in the Worcester pavilion as well. The W. G. Grace portrait is dated 1890 and the photograph of Sir Donald Bradman shows him batting at Worcester, his most prolific ground in England, on 30 April 1938, with fourteen thousand spectators present. The trophy cabinet contains not only Worcester's Britannic Assurance Championship trophies for 1988 and 1989, and their Refuge Assurance titles in 1987 and 1988, but also Roly Jenkins' Worcester Colts cap from 1936 and a block of glass with a metal plate attached reading: 'The Haniel Challenge. Winner Worcestershire County Cricket Club v The President's XI, April 11th 1989, Kowloon Cricket Club, Hong Kong.' Well, you've got to find somewhere to play if your ground is under several feet of river, and if you can bring back a tasteless trophy as well, so much the better.

Conclusion

SO THAT'S it. The tour has finished. For every pavilion finally included in the collection, I have been told about at least six more, all of which I was assured are unique, interesting, wonderful or horrible – and in many cases, I discovered, knocked down five years ago. I have been in pavilions where a deep respectful silence is the norm, and in others where the laughter barely ever stops. There are some where women are still not allowed, and many more where without women the whole place would fall apart. Some are home for Rotary Clubs every Wednesday, and others are so small that not even eleven cricketers can fit in at the same time. They are all beautiful to somebody, even though in some cases it is a beauty expressed more spiritually than physically.

The statistics are startling. We have come across more than forty pool tables, sixty-two televisions and hundreds of trophies, covering a variety of skills including golf, darts and gardening. We have noted four quite separate ways of protecting the windows from flying cricket balls (chicken wire, shutters, reinforced Triplex glass and sightscreens), and have seen at least five hundred paintings, photographs, busts and tea towels featuring a likeness of Dr W. G. Grace.

My summer tour has proved what I had already suspected. Cricket pavilions are not just architecture and statistics, they are not microcosms of the British way of life. They are just places where cricket lives. I was not on a voyage of discovery, nor on a nostalgic journey to bring back happy memories of days when the world was a bit younger. It was just meant to be fun.